How to Improve Your IQ

Published by :
Lotus Press Publishers & Distributors

How to Improve Your IQ

Bhawna Sharma

4735/22, Prakash Deep Building
Ansari Road, Darya Ganj,
New Delhi - 110002

Lotus Press : Publishers & Distributors
Unit No. 220, 2nd Floor, 4735/22, Prakash Deep Building,
Ansari Road, Darya Ganj, New Delhi- 110002
Ph.: 41325510, 98118-38000
• E-mail : lotuspress1984@gmail.com
www.lotuspress.co.in

How to Improve Your IQ

ISBN: 978-81-8382-260-2

Printed & Published by : **Lotus Press Publisher & Distributors,** New Delhi-02

PREFACE

You might have heard people, especially those in the corporate world, talking about IQ.

Have you ever wondered what is IQ? In simple terms, IQ stands for 'Intelligence Quotient'. It is a numerical score based on standardized tests that measure intelligence. It is considered a general indicator of intelligence.

German psychologist, William Stern saw the intelligence tests developed by psychologists Alfred Binet and Theodore Simon, and coined the term 'intelligence quotient' in 1912.

Binet and Simon had formed the tests to identify students that needed special help with the school curriculum.

In the present scenario, intelligence is highly appreciated. A person having a high IQ, has a better chance of becoming successful in different areas of practical life.

Several studies indicate different areas that affect an individual's IQ. Till a few years back, scientists believed that the IQ of an individual is genetic and cannot be improved upon. However, various researches by eminent scientists and neuropsychologists have proven this myth wrong.

They suggest some simple exercises to help improve IQ. These exercises include writing, reading, watching fiction, changing hobbies, solving puzzles, playing competitive games, breaking routines, exchanging cultural views, debating, teaching, etc.

The present book is written as a help for readers who want to improve their IQ. To start with, they should understand that it is not an uphill task.

We need a little training to utilize our brain in a manner better than what we are doing now. Apart from telling how IQ works and how it is measures, the different chapters of the book will help the readers exercise their brains in different manners in order to improve it.

Author

CONTENTS

CHAPTER 1

Meaning of Intelligence Quotient

Having a high Intelligence Quotient is a matter of pride and everybody wants that. The acronym for intelligent quotient is IQ.

IQ refers to a score given for several standardized intelligence tests designed to assess intelligence. Not all intelligence can be measured by an IQ test. An IQ test measures mathematical and spatial reasoning, logical ability, and language understanding.

Thus a person who is speaking English as a second language might score poorly on the language comprehension aspects of a test, and an IQ test would not be an adequate measurement of intelligence.

Moreover, an IQ test does not measure things like life experience, wisdom, or personal qualities like being a good friend or a devoted spouse. So it is not a predictor of a person's quality or worth, though it has occasionally been used as such. Some things can negatively impact IQ score.

These include malnutrition in children, who are tested, and fetal alcohol syndrome, or maternal addiction. Mental retardation or conditions that deteriorate the brain's capacity to remember like Alzheimer's disease also causes IQ scores to be lower. IQ may also be impacted by lack of appropriate education, often due to disparity in educational funding. If these disparities are corrected, then IQ scores normally increases.

The first of the IQ tests was developed by French psychologist Alfred Binet in 1905. He constructed the IQ test, as it would later be called, to determine which children might need additional help in scholarly pursuits.

Today, the IQ test is commonly based on some model of the Stanford Binet Intelligence scale.

Further, the term 'IQ,' which is taken from the German Intelligenz-Quotient, was devised by the German psychologist William Stern in 1912 as a proposed method of scoring children's intelligence tests such as those developed by Alfred Binet and Théodore Simon in the early 20th century. Lewis Terman accepted that form of scoring, expressing a score as a quotient of 'mental age' and 'chronological age,' for his revision of the Binet-Simon test, the first version of the Stanford-Binet Intelligence Scales.

Furthermore, the IQ test is controversial because it supposedly measures how intellectually bright one person is in comparison with the rest of the population. The first IQ (Intelligence Quotient) test originated in France and was the work of Alfred Binet who sought to find a way to differentiate between normal children and children who were struggling at school. It was later revised by Lewis Terman in the US and the Stanford-Binet IQ test was born.

More importantly, the term "IQ" is still in common use, the scoring of modern IQ tests such as the Wechsler Adult Intelligence Scale is now based on standard scoring of the subject's rank order on the test item content with the median score set to 100, and a standard deviation of 15, although not all tests adhere to that assignment of 15 IQ points to each standard deviation.

IQ scores have been shown to be associated with such factors as morbidity and mortality, parental social status and to a substantial degree, parental IQ. While the heritability of IQ has been investigated for nearly a century, controversy remains regarding the significance of heritability estimates and the mechanisms of inheritance are still a matter of some debate. IQ scores are used in many contexts: as predictors of educational achievement or special needs, by social scientists who study the distribution of IQ scores in populations and the relationships between IQ score and other variables, and as predictors of job performance and income.

The average IQ scores for many populations have been rising at an average rate of three points per decade since the early 20th century, a phenomenon called the Flynn effect. It is disputed whether these changes in scores reflect real changes in intellectual abilities, or merely methodological problems with past or present testing.

More likely, many people misunderstand the IQ scoring system which works on the principle that a score of 100 is average. A higher score means one is above average in comparison with the rest of the population and a score of less than 100 indicates that one is lower than average. It is reckoned that about half of the population will score between 90 and 110 on a standard IQ test.

As a rough guide, the following scores indicate scores in relation to the rest of the population.

- Over 130 – Extremely bright, only 2% of the population achieve this score
- Between 120 and 130 – Very bright, probably around 7% of the population

- Between 110 and 120 – Bright, 16% of the population
- Between 90 and 110 – Average, makes up about half the population so 50%
- Between 80 and 90 – Low average, 16%
- Between 70 and 80 – Borderline, 7%
- Lower than 70 – Extremely low, about 2%

A word of warning however. Intelligence depends on many factors such as environment, community, genetics, background etc.

It is worth remembering that Einstein himself was not considered 'intelligent' by any standard whilst at school.

More interesting, Intelligence Quotient is a measure of intellectual capacity. Intelligence is then assessed based on your individual score on an intelligence test—a score ranging between zero and 150+. The average adult's IQ score is 100, though a 15-point difference (a score of 85 or 115) is considered average as well; lower IQ scores indicate below average IQs, and higher IQ scores indicate above average IQs.

A variety of intelligence tests developed over the years; however, the most commonly used tests are the Stanford-Binet Scale of Intelligence, the Wechsler Adult Intelligence Scale (WAIS) and the Wechsler Intelligence Scale for Children (WISC).

IQ tests originated in France when Alfred Binet was asked by French government to create a testing system for intelligence—one that would separate the less intelligent children from the normally intelligent children. This led to the development of a test known as the Stanford Revision of the Binet-Simon Scale of Intelligence (commonly referred to as the Stanford-Binet).

For testing children, the Wechsler Intelligence Scale for Children is now in its fourth edition. Known as the WISC-IV, this test is designed for children aged 6 months to 16 years and 11 months.

Children's IQ is mostly determined by their scores in verbal comprehension, perceptual reasoning through pictures, the ability to memorise and recall numbers, and how fast they process and organise information during tasks.

Children's age are taken into consideration when measuring for IQ. The Wechsler Preschool and Primary Scale of Intelligence (WPPSI) is used as well; however, it is limited to use for children between ages 2 1/2 through 7 1/4.

In adults, the Wechsler Adult Intelligence Scale (WAIS) is the most commonly used IQ test for adults. Much like the WISC, the WAIS is in its fourth edition. The WAIS-IV is designed for individuals aged 16 and over. It measures verbal reasoning in addition to how well the individual interprets pictures, remembers and recalls numbers, and processes patterns and designs.

This test is often used in academic and clinical settings, where an individual can benefit in a number of ways. Academically, this may include placement in advanced or specialized classes; clinically, measuring a person's IQ can advise a clinician on how to approach diagnosis and treatment.

Furthermore, IQ tests provide valuable information regarding cognitive abilities. However, take into consideration age, culture and socioeconomic status when interpreting your IQ scores, as IQ scores do not always account for these factors.

Also, IQ is a measure of one's cognitive ability, and is not a predictor of how well a person will perform in school or work. Intelligence tests measure your abilities and the intellectual capacity you are born with, while achievement tests (such as the SAT) measure attainment and achievement. Do not assume that a poor score on a standardized test translates into low intelligence.

Intelligence testing is used to assess the all around effectiveness of an individual's mental processes, especially understanding, reasoning, and the ability to recall information. Tests exist that are appropriate for both children and adults. The use of standardized tests to produce a numerical value for these abilities is a very popular tool among educators.

Correctly administered, some intelligence tests can also detect learning impairments. The Stanford-Binet Intelligence Scale and the Wechsler Intelligence Scales are the two most widely used standardized intelligence tests.

Other tests are available that attempt to quantify areas such as creativity, personality, and ability or aptitude to perform specific tasks. Many employers, from police departments to sports league, use some form of standardized intelligence testing to evaluate job applicants.

■■■

CHAPTER 2

Steps to Increase IQ

In order to increase intelligence quotients, one can work on various factors that are helpful in improving and increasing the ability of brain to work. However, improving IQ is not a single day's work . It takes time in enhancing the intelligence quotient. Very true in this context, "Slow and steady, win the race".

Brain needs exercise just like muscles. If it is used in the right ways, it will become a more skilled thinker and increase ability to focus. But if it is not in use or is abused with harmful chemicals, the ability to think and learn will deteriorate.

Having a better IQ score will not always mean one has a more successful life. But determining intelligence is the only effective and objective way to predict professional success. Having an average IQ means one belongs to the majority of the population. It isn't that bad to have an average intelligence. But it isn't that good also. However, you don't have to feel so hopeless because your average IQ can still be improved. One can become an above average or even superior intelligent individual too.

An average intelligence means that you have an IQ score

between 90 and 109. About 50% of the population has an average IQ score. The rest of the population is distributed among high average, superior, very superior, low average, borderline, and extremely low intelligence. Having an average IQ score may be transformed to the professional success you may have.

According to a study, people who have an IQ score of 90 may become laborers, upholsterers, gardeners, farmhands, factory sorters and packers, and miners. Those with an IQ score of 100 usually become warehousemen, cooks, bakers, carpenters, small farmers, and van or truck drivers.

Meanwhile, people with an IQ score above 100 but less than 110 are more successful being machine operators, butchers, shopkeepers, metal workers, and welders. People with an IQ score of 110 can be foremen, telephone operators, clerks, policemen, accountants, and electricians. Although one may have an average IQ score, one can still enjoy and be successful in higher professions like being surgeons, scientists, accountants, engineers, and professors.

Following are some of the steps or factors that lead to improve our IQ. These are:

- *Concentration:* Watching and observing things carefully with concentration make the brain to exercise and helps in doing things wisely.
- *Open mind for new ideas:* Every time looks for new things around and doing new things helps in enhancing the brain activity that leads to improving the IQ.
- *Reading:* Reading enhances the mind's ability to comprehend, as well as encouraging thinking critically. Reading a book that has never read before broadens horizons, thus increasing IQ. Reading different genres is even more productive, as well as reading newspapers,

current events magazines, and multi-content periodicals. Make sure the book is in reading level and not something that is too easy.

- *Don't give up:* Ignore limiting stereotypes such as 'An old dog cannot learn new tricks'. Imagine the success you will feel when you bump up ten points. Soon enough, that fantasy will become a reality.
- *Try writing with opposite hand:* Writing with your opposite hand can in fact lead to stimulation of the side of the brain that is opposite to that hand. So perhaps a southpaw could go righty and think more logical, or a righty could try going left-handed to be more creative. However, keep in mind this is only a theory.
- *Write whenever possible:* Send a note instead of an email, or write a draft of a paper. It will increase visual and kinesthetic stimulation.
- *Play video games:* Games can be a great way to stimulate the brain. Try to play a game that is out of usual range of choices. It will help in thinking differently. Especially look for games that provide with problems to solve or force you to think quickly.
- *Work on cryptology:* This is when a message is written in codes and tries to figure it out. It's challenging for some, but after a while may even become enjoyable. All logic puzzles are great.
- *Practice crosswords and sudoku:* These activities stimulate mind and thought processes. People may not normally consider word searches thought-provoking, but if practiced in addition to other mind games, they could prove to be easy and stimulating.

- *Do logic and lateral thinking puzzles:* These help brain think outside the box and solve problems in different ways.
- *Take a weekly IQ test and record your results:* Consider placing the results on a line graph using excel or another graph-compatible programme.
- *Listen to classical music:* The Mozart effect suggests that by listening to classical music, a short-term improvement is induced on the performance of certain tasks. Gradually, this may have a somewhat long-term effect.
- *Excel in school and have a better career:* There is a huge amount of evidence substantiating the correlation between excellent grade and better intelligence. Good grades are the path to better careers and better ways of life.
- *Eat brain food:* Fish is one such brain food. However, avoid fish such as Tuna, as it often contains a high amount of mercury. Also try an Omega 3 or fish oil supplement. These also have great effects on health.
- *Exercise:* This increases blood flow to the brain-resulting also in increased thought/IQ. Using body clears head and creates a wave of energy. Afterwards, one feel invigorated and can concentrate more easily.
- *Sleep:* In order to store information into the long-term IQ, one needs to get enough sleep to transfer the short-term into the long-term. Just remember, it is a proven fact that sleeping longer stores more information into the long-term IQ.
- Use a Rubik's Cube, 15-puzzle, or other toy to pass the time instead of watching TV.
- Play games like chess and crossword puzzles. They help to think and it can be fun at the same time.

- Take nice, slow deep breaths when in thought.
- Do cardiovascular exercise and cut down on fatty foods to circulate the blood flow to brain.
- *Minimize Television Watching:* The problem is watching television doesn't use mental capacity OR allows it to recharge. It's like having the energy sapped out of a muscle without the health benefits of exercise.

  When feel like relaxing, try reading a book instead. If too tired, listen to some music. When with friends or family, leave the tube off and have a conversation. All of these things use mind more than television and allow relaxing.
- *Read Challenging Books:* If one wants to improve thinking and writing ability one should read books that make focus. Reading a classic novel can change view of the world and will make think in more precise, elegant English. Don't be afraid to look up a word if you don't know it, and don't be afraid of dense passages. Take time, re-read when necessary, and soon grow accustomed to the author's style. The challenge of learning new ideas is far more exciting than any tacky suspense-thriller.
- *Early to Bed, Early to Rise:* Nothing makes it harder to concentrate than sleep deprivation. If stay up late and compensate by sleeping late, one wake up lethargic and have trouble focusing. The early morning hours are the most tranquil and productive. Waking up early gives more productive hours and maximizes mental acuity all day.
- *Take Time to Reflect:* Often our lives get so hectic that we become overwhelmed without even realizing it. It becomes difficult to concentrate because nagging thoughts keep interrupting. Spending some time alone in reflection gives you a chance organise your thoughts and prioritize your

responsibilities. Afterwards, you'll have a better understanding of what's important and what isn't. The unimportant stuff won't bother you anymore and your mind will feel less encumbered.

- *Listen to Mozart:* Researchers found that children who studied piano and sang daily in chorus, were much better at solving puzzles, and when tested, scored 80% higher in spatial intelligence than the non-musical group. In another study, 36 students were given three spatial reasoning tests on a standard IQ test.
- *Avoid foods that cause subtle allergies:* These can include wheat, corn, peanuts and dairy products. Watch yourself to see if one have a problem with any of these. They cause digestive problems and brain fog in some people.
- *Speed reading:* When scanning, read the first and last parts of paragraphs; this is where the important stuff is. Just pick up any book or article now to verify this.
- *Exercise:* Long-term exercise can boost brainpower, which isn't surprising. Anything that affects physical health in a positive way probably helps the brain too. Recent research, though, shows that cognitive function is improved immediately after just ten minutes of aerobic exercise. If you need a brain recharge, one might want to walk up and down the stairs a few times.
- *Learn more efficiently:* When you decide to learn something, take notes from the start. Leave each "learning session" with a question or two in mind, to create anticipation and curiosity. Take short breaks, so there will be more beginnings and endings to studies. Things learned at the beginning or ending of a class or session are remembered better.

- *Use techniques for clear thinking:* Cluttered rooms and offices can contribute to cluttered thinking. Organize a space for mental work. Sigh, stretch, and take a deep breath before start on a tough mental job. Plan some distraction-free time for brainstorming.
- *Brain wave entrainment:* The newest brain wave entrainment products are powerful tools for altering brain function. Some will almost immediately relax, while others will put brain waves in a pattern that is most conducive to analytical thinking.
- *Creatine:* This is a compound found in meat, used by athletes to help build muscle. Now the evidence is here to show that it helps your brain as well. Proceedings B, a journal published by the Royal Society, reports that the research showed improvement in working IQ and general intelligence resulting from creatine supplementation. The dose used in the study was 5 grams per day. This is about the level used to boost sports performance, and is as much as you'd normally get in four pounds of meat, according to lead researcher Dr. Caroline Rae.
- *Talk:* Talking is only good for the brain if one is actually exercising it, of course. Try explaining something that one doesn't understand very well to a friend, though, and notice that the process of explaining will help clarify understanding.
- *Do something enjoyable:* This is a way to both lower stress and rev up your brain. The key is to do something active. Watching TV doesn't count. Whether it is playing Scrabble or building birdhouses, when you are actively engaged in an activity that you enjoy, you worry less about things and you start to think better.

- *Adjust beliefs:* Believing one is smarter, and one'll become smarter. For this, affirmations may work, but even better is evidence. Make a note of your successes. Tell yourself, "Hey, that was really creative," when you do something creative. When you have a good idea, make a note of it. Gather the evidence for your own intelligence and you'll start to experience more of it.

- *Brain exercises:* Do math in mind while driving. Think of a new use for everything you see. Almost any brain exercises have the potential to improve IQ and brain function. Regular use of the brain has been shown to generate new neuronal growth, and even halt the decline of mental function that often comes with age.

- *Model others:* Find others that are creative, intelligent, or very productive. Do what they do, and think what they think. This is a key principle of neuro-linguistic programming. Be careful about taking their advice, though. Successful people often don't really understand why they are successful. Do what they do, not what they say.

- *Eat fish:* Eating fish actually speeds up brain waves, and improves concentration. Researchers have also found an almost perfect correlation between intake of fish and lowered levels of depression in the various countries of the world. The U.S. has 24 times the incidence of depression as Japan, for example, where fish intake is much higher.

- *Avoid unnecessary arguments:* When defend a position too vigorously, especially when it is just to "win" the argument, one invest our ego into it. This is not conducive to the easy acceptance and use of new information. In other words, one put its mind in a rut, and dig it deeper with each argument. Debate can be a valuable thing, but when the ego takes over, the mind closes a little. This is not a way to improve IQ.

- *Breath deep:* More air in means more oxygen in the blood and therefore in the brain. Breathing through nose helps in using diaphragm more, drawing air deeper into lungs. Several deep breaths can also help to relax, which is conducive to clearer thinking.
- *Meditate:* A simple meditation can do right now is just closing eyes and paying attention to breath. Tensing up muscles and then relaxing them to start may help. When mind wanders, just bring attention back to your breath. Five or ten minutes of this will usually relax, clear mind, and leave more ready for any mental task.
- *Sit up straight:* Posture affects thinking process. Doing math while sitting up straight, keeping mouth closed and looking forward or slightly upwards helps in better intelligence.
- *Phosphotidyl Serine (PS):* This supplement has been shown in clinical studies to increase lucidity and rate of learning. It activates cell-to-cell communication, helps regulate cell growth, improves the functioning of the special receptors found on cells, and prepares cells for activity. In other words, it can help your brain power. It's also thought to reverse IQ decline. Phosphatidyl Serine has no known adverse side effects.
- *Vinpocetine:* This extract, derived from an alkaloid found in the Periwinkle plant, is used as a cerebral vasodilator. It increases blood flow to the brain, which improves its oxygenation and thereby increases mental alertness and acuity. Research suggests it may also be the most powerful IQ enhancer available to date.
- *Gingko Biloba:* The leaves of this tree have been proven to

increase blood flow to the brain. The trees are often planted in parks.

- *Saint John's Wort:* This is a common weed that may be growing in yard. Although it's brain enhancing qualities are less documented, many people swear by it's temporary mood-elevating effect, and our brains tend to function better when we are happy. Hyperacum Perforatum, is it's botanical name.
- *Good thinking habits:* Just use a problem solving technique for several weeks and it will become a habit. Redesign everything for a while, and that will become a habit. One can develop many good thinking habits with some effort, and then be more resourceful effortlessly from that point on. Use the power of habit.
- *Use dead time:* This is time that is otherwise wasted or just under-utilised. Driving time, time spent in waiting rooms, or even time spent raking yard can be included in this. With a tape player and a trip to a public library, start to use this time to listen to books-on-tape.
- *Learn a language:* Learning a new language has been shown to halt the age-related decline in brain function. It also introduces your mind to new concepts and new ways of looking at things. It is one of the best brain exercises.
- *Rosemary:* This common herb may have an effect on the brain when the scent is inhaled. We are waiting for the research, but some people swear that just sniffing rosemary wakes up their brain.
- *Mindfulness exercises:* Concentration and clear thinking are more or less automatic once you remove distractions. Learn to stop and watch your busy mind. As you notice things that are subtly bothering you, deal with them. This

might mean making a phone call you need to make, or putting things on a list so you can forget them for now. With practice, this becomes easier, and your thinking becomes more powerful.

- *Write:* Writing is good for your mind in a number of ways. It is a way to tell IQ what is important, so you'll recall things more easily in the future. It is a way to clarify your thinking. It is a way to exercise your creativity and analytical ability. Diaries, idea-journals, poetry, note-taking and story-writing are all ways to use writing to boost your brain power.
- *Develop intuition:* Intuition can be an important part of brainpower. Einstein and others have relied heavily on their intuitive hunches.
- *Sleep better:* As long as you get a certain amount of sleep probably a minimum of five hours – the quality seems to be more important than the quantity. Also, short naps in the afternoon seem to work well to recharge the brain for some people.
- *Caffeine:* The research shows higher test scores for students who drink coffee before major exams. In other studies, it has been shown that too much caffeine leads to poorer quality decisions. Caffeine affects individuals differently, and has some nasty long-term side effects for some of us, but short-term – it works!
- *Avoid sugar:* Any simple carbohydrates can give you 'brain fog'. Sometimes called the 'sugar blues' as well, this sluggish feeling makes it hard to think clearly. It results from the insulin rushing into the bloodstream to counteract the sugar rush. Avoid pasta, sugars, white bread and potato chips before any important mental tasks.
- *Hypnosis audios:* The power of suggestion is real, and one

way to use it is with hypnosis tapes, CD's or downloads. This type of brain 'programming' has more evidence for it than subliminals.

- *Imaginary friends:* Talking to and getting advice from characters in your mind can be a great way to access the information in your subconscious mind. Imagine a conversation with a person who has a lot of knowledge in the area you want advice in.
- *Develop creativity:* Creativity gives power to think. Raw computation can be done by computers now, but humans provide the creative thought that shapes our world.
- *Creatine:* This is a compound found in meat, used by athletes to help build muscle. Now the evidence is here to show that it helps your brain as well. Proceedings B , a journal published by the Royal Society reports that the research showed improvement in working IQ and general intelligence resulting from creatine supplementation. The dose used in the study was 5 grams per day. This is about the level used to boost sports performance, and is as much as you'd normally get in four pounds of meat, according to lead researcher Dr. Caroline Rae.
- *Laugh:* The release of endorphins caused by laughter lowers stress levels, which is good for long-term brain health. Laughter also tends to leave you more open to new ideas and thoughts.
- *Play:* Stimulating the brain causes measurable changes in the structure of the brain. New connections are made and new brain cells are grown. Intellectual play, as well as any playing that involves hand-eye coordination stimulates the brain.
- *Do puzzles:* Crossword puzzles, lateral thinking puzzles, and even good riddles are a great way to get brain exercise.

You can work on them while waiting for a dentist appointment, or on the bus, if you are short on time.

- *Sing:* When you are alone in your car, try singing about something you are working on. This taps into and exercises your right brain. Have you ever noticed how it is easier to rhyme when you sing than when you just speak or write?

  This is because the right brain is better at pattern recognition. By doing this brain exercise regularly you can train yourself to tap into the power of the right brain. This will make you a more effective problem-solver. If you doubt the distinction between the hemispheres of the brain, look at how stutterers can stop stuttering as soon as they start singing. Try it.

- *Nuts:* University students in Brazil and other South American countries often eat several Brazil nuts before an exam, believing they are good for their mental power. The evidence is starting to confirm this.

  Other nuts that have minerals and amino acids that are beneficial to the brain include almonds and walnuts.

- *Olive oil:* High in mono-unsaturated fat, olive oil has been shown to improve IQ. A cheaper alternative is canola oil, but this hasn't been studied much yet.

- *Vitamin supplements:* In studies, children scored higher on tests when on a regimen of daily vitamin supplements. "Experts" will tell you that if you eat a balanced diet, you don't need supplements, which, given the culture here, is really just a sales pitch for vitamins, isn't it? Who eats a perfectly balanced diet?

- *Fibre:* It isn't just what goes in, but what comes out that is important to brain function. Toxic build-up in the body and brain can cause "brain fog." People often report clearer thinking as one of the benefits of curing their constipation.

- *Self-awareness:* This may not seem important to brain power, but it is. When you know yourself better, you can avoid the usual effects of ego and emotion in your seemingly "rational" thinking.

  Or you can at least take it into account. Watch yourself, especially as you explain things or argue.

- *Motivate yourself:* Motivation is as important to mental tasks as it is to any other. Learn a few simple techniques for self motivation.

- *Avoid too much stress:* Neuropsychiastrist Richard Restak, M.D., from the George Washington University School of Medicine and Health Services, sums up the research thus: "Stress causes brain damage." Long-term stress has repeated been shown to hurt the brain, not to mention the rest of the body. Learn a few stress reduction techniques if you get stressed out often.

- *Get educated:* Scientists have known for a while that the less educated get alzheimer's more frequently. Education in any area seems to make the brain stronger.

- *Avoid too much fat:* In laboratory studies, animals consistently learn slower when they are on a diet high in fat. Type of fat may make a difference, so you may want to stick to using olive oil and other non-saturated fats. Saturated fats have been shown to actually stunt the growth of brain cells.

- *Eat less:* Overeating has the immediate effect of redirecting more blood to the digestive process, leaving less for the brain.

Long-term, it can cause arterial obstructions that reduce blood flow to the brain permanently. In at least one study, rats on a restricted-calorie diet had more brainpower.

- *Avoid suspect foods:* There is evidence that the following foods can be bad for your brain: Artificial food colourings, artificial sweeteners, colas, corn syrup, frostings, high-sugar drinks, hydrogenated fats, sugars, white bread, and any white-flour products.
- *Eat breakfast:* When kids who didn't eat breakfast started to eat it, researchers found that their math scores went up a whole grade on average.
- *Avoid diabetes:* The development of diabetes coincides with a dropping of IQ scores. In other words, if you want to maintain your brain power, follow your doctors dietary recommendations for preventing or treating diabetes.
- *Eat foods high in antioxidants*: Antioxidants protect all your cells, including brain cells. Some of the foods highest in antioxidants include: prunes, raisins, blueberries, blackberries, garlic, kale, cranberries, strawberries, spinach, and raspberries. In one test, rats had age-related mental decline reversed by eating the equivalent of a 1/2 cup of blueberries per day.
- *Use alcohol in moderation:* In a study at the University of Indiana School of Medicine, elderly light drinkers (fewer than 4 drinks per week) scored higher on tests of thinking abilities than non-drinkers.

  Those who drank 10 or more drinks per week scored lower. It is known that alcohol can kill brain cells, so moderation seems to be the key.
- *Folic acid:* According to one study, 200 micrograms of folic

acid, the amount found in 3/4 cup of cooked spinach, alleviates depression and reverses IQ loss.

- *Potential brain foods:* Other foods that may be good for your brain include: Avocados, bananas, lean beef, brewer's yeast. broccoli, brown rice, brussel sprouts, cantaloupe, cheese, chicken, collard greens, eggs, flaxseed oil, legumes, oatmeal, oranges, peanut butter, peas, potatoes, romaine lettuce, salmon, soybeans, spinach, tuna, turkey, wheat germ, and yogurt.
- *Vitamin E:* It is an antioxidant, and reduces the clogging of blood vessels, including those going in the brain.
- *Vitamin C:* Taken in the form of orange juice in a study at the Texas Women's University, vitamin C increased the IQ scores of children.
- *Selenium:* 100 micrograms of selenium has been shown to be a mood-elevator.

  Your brain almost certainly functions better when you are in a better mood. Foods rich in selenium include Brazil nuts and garlic.
- *Alpha-lipoic acid:* Alpha-lipoic acid (10 to 50 milligrams daily) improves IQ and protects nerve cells.
- *Inositol:* This is a safe and natural substance that is often grouped with the B-vitamins. It reduces stress and promotes clear thinking. It contributes to energy production, and so can "wake you up." Animal studies show a measurable increase in physical activity for up to five hours after taking it.
- *Huperzine A:* This is a compound extracted from the Chinese club moss. Researchers both in Israel and the U.S. have used it to treat alzheimer's. It improves IQ and learning an seems to be very safe.

- *Sniff basil:* This another of the herbs that may be good for brain. No studies yet, but many report a brain boost from smelling basil.
- *Temperature:* Many people have noted that they think better at certain temperatures. In general, it seems that being slightly cool, but not uncomfortable, is most conducive to good thinking.
- *Use systems:* One can find own easier ways to do mental math or other mental tasks, or read a good book on them.
- *Make a brainpower plan:* It takes about twenty to thirty days of repetition to establish new habits, many psychologists will tell. This means that when create plan for better brainpower, be sure plan to use that new problem solving technique, or eat those new brain' foods for at least three weeks.
- *Practice makes higher IQ score:* Usually, one can get a higher IQ score the second or third time you take the test. So maybe, just maybe, practicing can help you get higher IQ score.
- *Take the test the smart way:* IQ tests are timed so better skip questions that are tough and answer first those that are easy. Never waste your time on a tough question. If you do, you pass up the chance to answer 5 questions correctly. Also, when you are answering a multiple choice type of test, eliminate answers that you suspect are incorrect. This will leave you fewer options and a better chance to get the right answer.
- *Learn the tricks to get higher IQ score:* Enough sleep proves to give higher intelligence. In fact, you can think better if you have had enough rest and sleep, especially prior to taking the test. Breathing deeply through your nose and

sitting up straight can also be a way to do well on IQ tests. Changing your diet like eating more fish may speed up your brain waves too and increase your level of concentration.

Many studies have been done to prove that music has an effect on a person's intelligence. So try listening to some Mozart music before the exam. One study shows that listening to this music for at least 10 minutes can increase your IQ score by nine points.

- *Do mental exercises:* Enjoy a longer-term of improved intelligence by doing mental exercises. Just as your body needs physical exercise in order for you to become strong, so does your brain needs exercise in order for it to remain sharp. Play mentally challenging games.

■■■

CHAPTER 3

Types of IQ and IQ Tests

Traditional intelligence tests usually measure the logical and mathematical components. However, there are actually 8 different kinds of IQ.

The Eight Types of Intelligence

1. *Linguistic and Verbal Intelligence:* If you excel in this type of category, you can be called word smart. Linguistic intelligence is how a person uses words and language to express and appreciate the meaning of things. If you're word smart, you could be a writer, journalist, an avid reader — or maybe you just like to solve crossword puzzles!
2. *Logical and Mathematical Intelligence:* Those who are good with numbers and computers have this type of intelligence, and they can be called number smart.
3. *Spatial Intelligence:* This type of intelligence refers to being picture smart wherein you typically use your active imagination, and graphic and artistic skills. Spatial intelligence is exhibited by artists, sculptors and architects.

4. *Body and Movement Intelligence:* You can be called body smart if you excel in this type of intelligence — where you have the ability to use a variety of physical skills.
5. *Musical Intelligence:* As the name implies, musical intelligence refers to a person's ability to create, appreciate and reproduce music.
6. *Interpersonal Intelligence:* This is when you can be called people smart. When you have this type of intelligence, you are able to understand and interact effectively with other people.
7. *Intrapersonal Intelligence:* There's also intrapersonal intelligence, which is exhibited by psychologists, philosophers and spiritual leaders. These are the people who have the ability to reflect on their inner thoughts and feelings.
8. *Naturalist Intelligence:* Finally, there are those who can be called nature smart. Hunters, farmers, environmentalists and animal lovers exhibit this type of intelligence, which involves the ability to discriminate among living things and be sensitive to nature.

Types of Intelligence Tests

A variety of intelligence tests developed over the years; however, the most commonly used tests are the Stanford-Binet Scale of Intelligence, the Wechsler Adult Intelligence Scale (WAIS) and the Wechsler Intelligence Scale for Children (WISC). IQ tests originated in France when Alfred Binet was asked by French government to create a testing system for intelligence—one that would separate the less intelligent children from the normally intelligent children. This led to the development of a test known as the Stanford Revision of the Binet-Simon Scale of Intelligence (commonly referred to as the Stanford-Binet).

For testing tests in children, the Wechsler Intelligence Scale for Children is now in its fourth edition. Known as the WISC-IV, this test is designed for children aged 6 months to 16 years and 11 months. Children's IQ is mostly determined by their scores in verbal comprehension, perceptual reasoning through pictures, the ability to memorise and recall numbers, and how fast they process and organise information during tasks. Children's ages are taken into consideration when measuring for IQ. The Wechsler Preschool and Primary Scale of Intelligence (WPPSI) is used as well; however, it is limited to use for children between ages 2 1/2 through 7 1/4.

In adults, the Wechsler Adult Intelligence Scale (WAIS) is the most commonly used IQ test for adults. Much like the WISC, the WAIS is in its fourth edition. The WAIS-IV is designed for individuals aged 16 and over. It measures verbal reasoning in addition to how well the individual interprets pictures, remembers and recalls numbers, and processes patterns and designs. This test is often used in academic and clinical settings, where an individual can benefit in a number of ways. Academically, this may include placement in advanced or specialized classes; clinically, measuring a person's IQ can advise a clinician on how to approach diagnosis and treatment.

The Stanford-Binet Intelligence Scale

Alfred Binet (1857-1911) was a French psychologist who was interested in the study of thinking and mental processes. As the director of physiological psychology at the Sorbonne, he was asked by the French Ministry of Public Instruction to develop a method of identifying children who were too so far below average in intelligence that they could not be educated in ordinary public schools. In 1905, Binet and his colleague,

Theodore Simon, developed a series of graded tasks that could be performed by children of average intelligence at different ages. During the next six years, until his death, Binet worked to refine this scale to produce a score that represented the mental age of the child.

Lewis Terman was studying the differences between groups of very bright and very dull students on various tests. Terman, who joined the faculty of Stanford University in 1910, adapted the Binet intelligence tests and coined the term IQ for intelligence quotient. This numberrepresented a ratio between the mental age and the chronological age of the child. Terman's modifications of Binet's tests became known as the Stanford-Binet test. This test and its subsequent revisions is the most widely used of all mental tests in the United States. The test is now in its fourth edition, sometimes refereed to as SB-FE. It is used to test people between the ages of 2 and 23.

The Stanford Binet test is administered individually, and to be accurate mustbe administered by a trained administrator, usually a psychologist or psychiatrist. It is routinely used as tools in school placement, in suggesting the possibility of a learning disability or a developmental delay, and in tracking intellectual development.

Although the Stanford-Binet scales have been expanded to include children asyoung as two, the test is not particularly reliable in screening very young children for developmental delays or disabilities. Young children are difficult test subjects because they are often wary of strangers, perform inconsistently in unfamiliar settings, have short attention spans, and are easily distractible.

The Sanford-Binet test cannot be used to diagnose mental retardation in children aged three and under, and the scoring design may not detect developmental problems in preschool-age children. For this reason, when evaluating very young children, the trend is toward a team assessment with many components rather than relying on a single test or IQ number.

It is no longer thought that IQ remains constant during a child's development. Not until around age five does the test start to distinguish children who are likely to show especially high or low intelligence as adults. However, IQ measured at age 12 tends to be in line with adult intelligence measures. The Stanford-Binet test does not necessarily predict how well a person will do in school or daily life. Too many factors besides raw intelligence, such as home environment, interest in learning, quality of school instruction, willingness to stick to a task, and support and mentoring from adults affect how well a person does in school and in future occupations.

The fourth edition of the Stanford-Binet Intelligence Scale that is currently in use was released in 1986. It was designed with a larger, more diverse, representative sample to Minimise the gender and racial inequities that had been criticized in earlier versions of the test.

The Stanford-Binet is a standardized test, meaning that norms, or average values, are established before the test is released for general use by administering the test to a large, representative sample of the prospective test population. The test population for the SR-FE consisted of over 5,000 people between the ages of 2 years and 23 years, 11 months. The test designers attempted to achieve a balance within the test population by considering geographical region, community size, race, ethnic identity, gender, parental occupation and parental education to address some of the concerns about inequality in earlier versions of the test.

The Stanford-Binet scale tests intelligence across four areas: verbal reasoning, quantitative reasoning, abstract/visual reasoning, and short-term IQ. The SB-FE differs from earlier versions of the test because it gives subtest scores in the four areas as well as a single composite IQ score. The areas are covered by 15 subtests, including vocabulary, comprehension, verbal absurdities, pattern analysis, matrices, paper folding and cutting, copying, quantitative, number series, equation building, IQ for sentences, IQ for digits, IQ for objects, and bead IQ.

All test subjects take an initial vocabulary test, which along with the subject's age, determines the number and level of subtests to be administered. Total testing time is 45-90 minutes, depending on the subject's age and the number of subtests given. Raw scores are based on the number of items answered, and are converted into a standard age score corresponding to age group. The mean, or average, score on the Stanford-Binet test is 100. This means 50 per cent of people score above 100 and 50 per cent score below 100. The actual number is calculated by taking the person's mental age as determined by the test results and dividing it by their chronological age then multiplying by 100. For example, if a 14 year old does as well as the average 16 year old, the IQ score is 16/14 x 100 = 114. Scores generally range from about 40 (very low) to 160 (very high). An IQ score of 130 is higher than about 98 per cent of all people tested.

The Wechsler Intelligence Scales

The Wechsler Intelligence Scales consist of several different standardized tests used to evaluate reasoning and intellectual abilities in pre-school children through adults.

David Wechsler (1896-1981) was an American psychologist who began his careerby administering and interpreting mental tests that had been designed for the United States Army to assign recruits to army jobs that best suited their abilities. Through these experiences, he expanded the definition of intelligence to include the global capacity to act purposefully, to think rationally, and to deal effectively with the environment. He believed that intelligence wasan aspect of personality, not a separate, isolated quality. Wechsler then developed intelligence tests to measure what he viewed as intelligence. Like the Stanford-Binet tests, the Wechsler tests are administered individually by a trained test administrator. Because they are easier to administer, these tests are often preferred by school psychologists over the Stanford-Binettests. There are currently three Wechsler Intelligence Scales in use in theUnited States today: The Wechsler Adult Intelligence Scale – Revised (WAIS-R), the Wechsler Intelligence Scale for Children-Third Edition (WISC-III), andthe Wechsler Preschool and Primary Scale of Intelligence - Revised (WPPSI-R).

The Wechsler scales are divided into six verbal and five performance subtests. The complete test takes 60-90 minutes to administer. Verbal and Performance IQs are scored based on the results of the testing, and then a composite Full Scale IQ score is computed. The Wechsler Adult Intelligence Scales are used to determine vocational ability, to assess adult intellectual ability in the classroom, and to determine organic deficits. Both adult and children's Wechsler scales, as well as the Stanford-Binet test, are often included in neuropsychological testing to assessthe brain function of individuals with neurological impairments.

The WAIS-R was revised in 1981 because of a need for a more contemporary norm group than the original test sample. The test is designed for adults, age 16-74. To establish the norms, or average values, for the revised version, the testwas given to a sample of 1,180 Americans. The sample included both Whites andpeople of colour who were able to speak and understand English. Excluded fromthe sample group were people who were institutionalized for mental retardation, who were brain damaged, who were severely emotionally disturbed, and who had restrictive physical disabilities. All the Wechsler tests have average orstandard scores of 100. People are compared against others in their age group.

The 11 subtests of the WAIS-R include information, digit span, vocabulary, arithmetic, comprehension, similarities, picture completion, picture arrangement, block design, object assembly, and digit symbol.

An example of questions on the subtest of similarities might be: "Describe how the following pair of words are alike or the same—hamburger and pizza." A correct response would be"Both are things to eat."

Wechsler Intelligence Scale for Children, Third Edition subtests include manyof the same categories of subtests as the WAIS-R. In addition, there are twooptional performance subtests: symbol search and mazes. The test is designedfor children ages 6 to 16. The test is divided into two main sections,.

The verbal section measures how well children express themselves in words and howwell they understand what others say to them. The performance section measures non-verbal areas such as spatial relationships.

Breaking down the tests into sections related to different kinds of learning is an advantage in helping psychologists detect patterns of strengths and weaknesses and in pinpointing learning disabilities.

Wechsler Preschool and Primary Scale of Intelligence-Revised was released in 1989. It is designed to assess the intelligence of children ages 3 through 7 years, 3 months.

This is an extension of the range of the original test, which was designed for children ages 4 years, 6 months through 6 years. The testis divided into six verbal and five performance subtests.

The eleven subtests are presented in the following order: information, animal house and animal house retest, vocabulary, picture completion, arithmetic, mazes, geometric design, similarities, block design, comprehension, and sentences. As with the other Wechsler tests, the average score is 100, and children are compared against the performance of other children their age.

Other intelligence tests also exist. One is the Slosson Intelligence Test-Revised (SIT-R), also called the "Short Intelligence Test." The revised versionwas issued in 1991. This test can be used from infancy through age 27, and contains items similar to the Wechsler scales.

One advantage is that the test does not have to be administered by a trained test giver. The disadvantage is that there are statistical and interpretive limitations on the data that comes out of the testing process.

Other Types of Intelligence Testing

Other tests are designed to be given in groups. These include the Cognitive Abilities Test (CAT) and the School and College Abilities Tests (SCAT). These tests can be given by untrained test administrators and are computer scored.

Intelligence testing is just one snapshot of a person's abilities. The information from the test does not predict one's success in life. It should be taken as just one factor in a complete neurological or psychiatric evaluation.

■■■

Chapter 4

Tests for Improving IQ

Stanford-Binet Intelligence Scale

The Stanford-Binet Intelligence Scale: Fourth Edition (SB: FE) is a standardized test that measures intelligence and cognitive abilities in children and adults, from age two through mature adulthood.

The Stanford-Binet Intelligence Scale was originally developed to help place children in appropriate educational settings. It can help determine the level of intellectual and cognitive functioning in preschoolers, children, adolescents and adults, and assist in the diagnosis of a learning disability, developmental delay, mental retardation , or giftedness. It is used to provide educational planning and placement, neuropsychological assessment, and research.

The Stanford-Binet Intelligence Scale is generally administered in a school or clinical setting.

The Stanford-Binet intelligence scale is used as a tool in school placement, in determining the presence of a learning disability or a developmental delay , and in tracking intellectual development. In addition, it is sometimes included in neuropsychological testing to assess the brain function of individuals with neurological impairments.

Further, the Stanford-Binet Intelligence Scale is considered to be one of the best and most widely used intelligence tests available. It is especially useful in providing intellectual assessment in young children, adolescents, and young adults. The test has been criticized for not being comparable for all age ranges. This is because different age ranges are administered different subtests. Additionally, for very young preschoolers, it is not uncommon to receive a score of zero due to test difficulty or the child's unwillingness to cooperate. Consequently, it is difficult to discriminate abilities in this age group among the lower scorers.

Administration and interpretation of results of the Stanford-Binet Intelligence Scale requires a competent examiner who is trained in psychology and individual intellectual assessment, preferably a psychologist.

The Stanford-Binet Intelligence Scale has a rich history. It is a descendant of the Binet-Simon scale which was developed in 1905 and became the first intelligence test. The Stanford-Binet Intelligence Scale was developed in 1916 and was revised in 1937, 1960, and 1986. The present edition was published in 1986. The Stanford Binet Intelligence Scale is currently being revised and the Fifth Edition is expected to be available in the spring of 2003.

Administration of the Stanford-Binet Intelligence Scale typically takes between 45 to 90 minutes, but can take as long as two hours, 30 minutes. The older the child and the more subtests administered, the longer the test generally takes to complete.

The Stanford-Binet Intelligence Scale is comprised of four cognitive area scores which together determine the composite score and factor scores. These area scores include: Verbal

Reasoning, Abstract/Visual Reasoning, Quantitative Reasoning, and Short-Term IQ. The composite score is considered to be what the authors call the best estimate of "g" or "general reasoning ability" and is the sum of all of subtest scores. General reasoning ability or "g" is considered to represent a person's ability to solve novel problems. The composite score is a global estimate of a person's intellectual functioning.

The test consists of 15 subtests, which are grouped into the four area scores. Not all subtests are administered to each age group; but six subtests are administered to all age levels. These subtests are: Vocabulary, Comprehension, Pattern Analysis, Quantitative, Bead IQ, and IQ for Sentences. The number of tests administered and general test difficulty is adjusted based on the test taker's age and performance on the sub-test that measures word knowledge. The subtest measuring word knowledge is given to all test takers and is the first subtest administered.

The following is a review of the specific cognitive abilities that the four area scores measure. The Verbal Reasoning area score measures verbal knowledge and understanding obtained from the school and home learning environment and reflects the ability to apply verbal skills to new situations. Examples of subtests comprising this factor measure skills which include: word knowledge, social judgment and awareness, ability to isolate the inappropriate feature in visual material and social intelligence, and the ability to differentiate essential from non-essential detail.

The Abstract/Visual Reasoning area score examines the ability to interpret and perform mathematic operations, the ability to visualise patterns, visual/motor skills, and problem-solving skills through the use of reasoning. An example of a subtest which determines the Abstract/Visual Reasoning score is a timed test that involves tasks such as completing a basic puzzle and replicating black and white cube designs.

The Quantitative Reasoning area score measures: numerical reasoning, concentration, and knowledge and application of numerical concepts. The Quantitative Reasoning area is combined with the Abstract/Visual Reasoning area score to create an Abstract/Visual Reasoning Factor Score.

The short-term IQ score measures concentration skills, short-term IQ, and sequencing skills. Subtests comprising this area score measure visual short-term IQ and auditory short term IQ involving both sentences and number sequences. In one subtest that measures visual short-term IQ, the participant is presented with pictures of a bead design, and asked to replicate it from IQ. The Stanford-Binet Intelligence Scale is a standardized test, which means that a large sample of children and adults were administered the exam as a means of developing test norms. The population in the sample was representative of the population of the United States based on age, gender, race or ethnic group, geographic region, community size, parental education, educational placement (normal versus special classes), etc. From this sample, norms were established. Norms are the performance of a comparison group of subjects—that nature of the group should be specified, and this usually constitutes a normal group so that the performance of the tested individual can be compared to this group and thus evaluated.

The numbers of correct responses on the given subtests are converted to a SAS score or Standard Age Score which is based on the chronological age of the test subject. This score is similar to an I.Q. score. Based on these norms, the Area Scores and Test Composite on the Stanford-Binet Intelligence Scale each have a mean or average score of 100 and a standard deviation of 16. For this test, as with most measures of intelligence, a score of 100 is in the normal or average range. The standard deviation indicates how above or below the norm a child's score is. For example, a score of 84 is one standard deviation below the norm score of 100. Based on the number of correct responses on a given subtest, an age-equivalent is available to help interpret the person's level of functioning.

Test scores provide an estimate of the level at which a child is functioning based on a combination of many different subtests or measures of skills. A trained psychologist is needed to evaluate and interpret the results, determine strengths and weaknesses, and make overall recommendations based on the findings and observed behavioral observations.

Test anxiety can have a negative impact on a child's performance, so parents should attempt to take the stress off their child by making sure they understand that it is the effort and attention they give the test, not the final score that matters. Parents can also ensure that their children are well-rested on the testing day and have a nutritious meal beforehand.

History of the Stanford-Binet Intelligence Scales

The study of the history of major psychological assessment instruments is hardly an active field. Most professionals view assessment instruments simply as practical tools of little interest beyond their immediate applied use. Nevertheless, when authors begin a revision of such an instrument, particularly when the instrument has already undergone a number of revisions, they are wise to examine the history of that assessment to provide continuity of measurement, to improve on the features, and to overcome limitations of earlier versions. In addition, understanding the history of a test may help the clinician compare the scores on the newest edition of the test to the scores on an earlier edition of thetest with which they are familiar.

The history of assessment instruments may also be of interest to historians of education, psychology, and science. Such interest would probably focus on an original approach to assessment and the subsequent development of that approach. Truly original assessment tools are rare. Such instruments, and their attendant theories, may have a sufficiently large impact on the field as to essentially spur a revolution in theory and application, along the lines of Kuhn's discussion of paradigm shifts in the history of science. A new assessment paradigm would begin with revolutionary fervor but would cool over time into "normal science." The history of intelligence measurement, and particularly Binet's major contribution, almost certainly qualifies as an original approach to assessment. As with other scientific revolutions described by Kuhn, Binet's initial contribution led to a period of revolutionary science followed by a drawn-out period of normal science, during which the original brilliant insight was improved gradually over time with steady and practical enhancements. Kuhn noted that although revolutionary science tends to grab the attention and the spotlight, normal science is what tends to be responsible for real progress, in both basic science and its applications. One can probably say the same for the history of intelligence tests and intelligence testing. This bulletin provides a history of the Stanford-Binet, beginning with its precursors in the work of Alfred Binet and Theodore Simon at the turn of the 20th century. Readers with a broader interest in the history of assessment instruments may also find the discussion of interest, although it is not the primary goal of this bulletin to provide the full history of intelligence testing in terms of a Kuhnian scientific revolution.

Test Structure

The Stanford-Binet is one of the first examples of an adaptive test. Examiners use the information they have about an examinee to determine where to begin testing and administer only those items that are appropriate for that examinee. This format reduces the time required to obtain reliable information from a test and decreases the frustration examinees experience when presented with items that are too hard or too easy. The use of multiple possible starting points, along with basal and ceiling rules, limits the time required to administer the test and maximizes the information obtained from each item.

One element of test structure that appears throughout the history of the Stanford-Binet is that of point scales and age scales. A point scale is the currently widespread arrangement of tests into subtests, with all items of a given type administered together. Age scales, long a part of the Stanford-Binet format, may not be familiar to the current generation of examiners. Initially, this format was used to provide a direct translation of the child's performance to mental age.

Psychometric as well as developmental information was used to place items on the test. Examinees experienced a variety of items that changed both quantitatively and qualitatively. Definitions, for example, went from concrete words to abstract words to the comparison of abstract words. The argument has often been made that this format is more engaging and provides a richer opportunity for the examiner to observe the examinee's performance. In 1916, Robert Yerkes began a series of debates with Lewis Terman on the appropriateness of the age scale. While Terman's methods prevailed at the time, the structure of many current tests shows the popularity of the point-scale subtest.

Throughout most of its history, the Stanford-Binet maintained a hybrid structure, combining point-scale and age-scale formats. Terman presented two parallel vocabulary scales in 1916, and every version of the Stanford-Binet except Form M has included a vocabulary scale. In 1986, the Fourth Edition of the book provided a standard method for using Vocabulary as a routing test to determine where to begin testing. Although this was the first formal mention of routing in a Stanford-Binet manual, using vocabulary for this purpose had been the unofficial practice of many examiners for decades. The Fifth Edition of the book includes a nonverbal routing test in addition to Vocabulary, and it uses performance on these subtests to route to the Nonverbal and Verbal age scales.

Verbal and Nonverbal Content

The verbal content of the Stanford-Binet has been of concern since the first publication in 1916, in which verbal items predominated. Subsequent revisions have attempted to better balance the verbal and nonverbal items, and McNemar reports that attempts were made to create a parallel nonverbal form in 1937. During the 1986 revision, the authors tried to create a nonverbal routing test using Matrices; however, sufficient low-end items were not created. While several nonverbal forms were recommended for different editions of the Stanford-Binet, the test never had a published nonverbal form prior to 2003.

The Fifth Edition provides an equal balance of verbal and nonverbal content within each factor. Norms are provided for Verbal IQ (VIQ) and Nonverbal IQ (NVIQ) scores as well as for Full Scale IQ (FSIQ), and the correlations between these scores range from .94 to .97 across the age range of the test.

Testing time and examinee fatigue have always been important issues for psychological assessment practitioners. Recognising that testing time might need to be reduced, Lewis Terman included instructions for a minimal level of lenience in establishing basal and ceiling performance. An examinee, he reasoned, could miss one item at an age level and still have a basal. Later, in 1937, instructions were included with the Stanford-Binet for the administration of an abbreviated test battery. With little loss of reliability, designated items could be omitted from the test to conserve time.

Remaining items administered in this fashion were given more weight in the calculation of IQ. This feature was retained in the 1960/1973 edition where, for instance, an examiner could omit IQ for Sentences and Copying a Bead Chain from IQ at age 13. The Fourth Edition of the book also allowed for an abbreviated administration through its flexible selection of subtests. Differen combinations of subtests were recommended for different purposes, including a four-test screening battery and a six-test screening battery. While these screeners do not allow for a good measure of an individual's pattern of abilities, they provide a quick measure of IQ. A similar method is used in the Fifth Edition, with Vocabulary and Object-Series/ Matrices providing the Abbreviated Battery IQ (ABIQ). The ABIQ, like the FSIQ, is equally weighted in terms of verbal and nonverbal content.

Reviews of the Stanford-Binet

Along with the extensive research literature on the Stanford-Binet, reviews of the test have been available since before the first Mental Measurement Yearbook was published. The content of these reviews has been distilled where possible in Table 6 to offer a summary of the advantages and possible limitations of the different versions of the test. The 1916 edition of the Stanford-Binet provided continuity with the Binet-Simon test, while at the same time expanding the range of items and providing a large research sample. The test offered only limited nonverbal content, provided only sparse instructions on scoring some items, and was not an adequate measure of adult intelligence. The 1937 editions again extended the range of items, provided a set of toys and objects to engage young children, and added more nonverbal content, predominantly at the lower end of the scale. This edition also improved the psychometric characteristics of the test by introducing a parallel form and more representative norms.

While better than the 1916 edition, Forms L and M were still criticized for the quality of the scoring rules, the paucity of nonverbal content at the upper levels of the test, and the non uniform standard deviation of IQ that led to different interpretations of IQ at different ages. This last point was corrected with the publication of the Form L-M, which provided tables to correct for this. Not only were the best items from the parallel 1937 forms used to create Form L-M, but also the ambiguities in scoring were cleared up, and the stimulus materials were presented in a much more convenient bound format. Some reviewers suggested that the format could be further improved by providing the scoring standards alongside the items in a single book. The test was also criticized for remaining heavily weighted with verbal materials, having what was perceived as an inadequate ceiling for adolescents and highly gifted examinees, and continuing to provide only a single measure of general intelligence.

The Fourth Edition of the book attempted to address many concerns that had been raised with prior versions of the test, while maintaining the same types of tasks and items. In particular, this version of the test offered several factor scores based on an explicit theoretical framework. This test introduced the easel format to the Stanford-Binet, providing both administration and scoring information as well as stimulus material in one place. The test featured higher ceilings for adolescents and over five times as many nonverbal items as the previous edition. Although the test provided for flexible administration, such a degree of flexibility can also lead to unneeded complexity. The test introduced creative extensions of classic items, but it lacked many of the toys and other interesting stimuli from the earlier editions. The continued use of a standard deviation of 16 was also criticized, as was the sample weighting done to approximate the characteristics of the general population.

The Fifth Edition is too new at this point to provide a list of possible limitations collected from the literature. Attempts were made to address the limitations of prior versions, while maintaining the advantages. Artwork and manipulative have been improved, and toys and game like materials were included. The SB5 does not allow for as many administrative options as the Fourth Edition; this makes for a more straightforward testing session. The Fifth Edition covers the widest age range of any Stanford-Binet (2 through 85+ years) and addresses the criticism about verbal content, norms, and the standard deviation.

Score/Test Comparability

With any newly revised test, questions arise about the relationship between scores and interpretations of the new version relative to the research and use of the prior editions. With the research tradition of the Stanford-Binet, it is especially important to provide these comparisons. The comparability of new and old forms, as well as the validity evidence reported in the Technical Manual for the Fifth Edition, provide the initial evidence for appropriate use of the test until independent research is published.

Test Structure

While early versions of the Stanford-Binet yielded only a general intelligence score, the items included a diverse mix of mental abilities. For example, items for age 4 of the 1916 edition contained visual-spatial (copying a square), quantitative (counting 4 pennies), knowledge (comprehension), and IQ (repeating 4 digits) items. Although the types of items at any level of the 1916 to 1973 versions varied, almost all items on these forms relate to knowledge, fluid reasoning, visual-spatial processing, quantitative reasoning, or short-term/working IQ. The Fourth Edition separated the diverse types of items found on prior editions into subtests and factors, grouping Visual-Spatial Processing and Fluid Reasoning together into an Abstract/Visual Reasoning factor. The Fifth Edition also maintains these five predominant areas of mental ability with a factor structure that keeps Fluid Reasoning items separate from Visual-Spatial Processing items. The Fifth Edition also places more emphasis on working IQ compared with short-term IQ.

While working IQ was present to some extent on earlier editions, it was limited to IQ for Digits Reversed, with all other IQ tasks involving short-term IQ.

These classifications are based on a content analysis of prior editions as well as on empirical studies. Of course, content analysis does not necessarily ensure that an item will load on a particular factor in a factor analysis, or that all practitioners will agree on the classifications given.

Conclusions

The Stanford-Binet Intelligence Scales, Fifth Edition represents the latest in a series of enhancements derived from the tradition of intelligence testing originated in 1905 by Alfred Binet and Theodore Simon. However, as Kuhn points out, the real progress in a science, and certainly the real progress in the fruits of a science, lies not in the revolutionary period but rather in the periods of normal science that follows it. According to Kuhn, "the results gained in normal research are significant because they add to the scope and precision with which the paradigm can be applied". The SB5 incorporates many insights implicitly designed into the early editions of the measure as implemented by Binet, Simon, Terman, and Merrill, but presents them in a way that provides vast practical improvements in the areas of content coverage and psychometric characteristics. In this way, the revolutionary work of the earlier authors has shaped the more recent enhancements and advancement of the test under Thorndike, Hagen, and Sattler, and most recently, Roid.

Wechsler Intelligence Tests

The Wechsler intelligence tests are a widely used series of intelligence tests developed by clinical psychologist David Wechsler. The Wechsler Intelligence Scales for Children and Wechsler Preschool and Primary Scale of Intelligence are used as tools in school placement, in determining the presence of a learning disability or a developmental delay, in identifying giftedness, and in tracking intellectual development. They are often included in neuropsychological testing to assess the brain function of individuals with neurological impairments.

The most distinctive feature of the Wechsler tests is their division into a verbal section and a nonverbal (or performance) section, with separate scores available for each subsection. All of the Wechsler scales are divided into six verbal and five performance subtests. The complete test takes 60 to 90 minutes to administer. Verbal intelligence, the component most often associated with academic success, implies the ability to think in abstract terms using either words or mathematical symbols. Performance intelligence suggests the ability to perceive relationships and fit separate parts together logically into a whole. The inclusion of the performance section in the Wechsler scales is especially helpful in assessing the cognitive ability of non-native speakers and children with speech and language disorders . The test can be of particular value to school psychologists screening for specific learning disabilities because of the number of specific subtests that make up each section.

The Wechsler Preschool and Primary Scales of Intelligence (WPPSI) have traditionally been geared toward children ages four to six years old, although the newest version of the test extends the age range down to three years and upward to seven years three months. The verbal section covers the following areas: general information (food, money, the body, etc.), vocabulary (definitions of increasing difficulty), comprehension (responses to questions), arithmetic (adding, subtracting, counting), sentences (repeating progressively longer sentences), and similarities (responding to questions such as "How are a pen and pencil alike?"). The performance section includes picture completion, copying geometric designs, using blocks to reproduce designs, working through a maze, and building an animal house from a model.

The Wechsler Intelligence Scale for Children (WISC) is designed for children and adolescents ages six to 16. Its makeup is similar to that of the Preschool Scale. Differences include the following: geometric designs are replaced by assembly of three-dimensional objects; children arrange groups of pictures to tell simple stories; they are asked to remember and repeat lists of digits; a coding exercise is performed in place of the animal house; mazes are a subtest. For all of the Wechsler scales (which also include the Wechsler Adult Intelligence Scale, or WAIS), separate verbal and performance scores, as well as a total score, are computed. These are then converted using a scale divided into categories (such as average and superior), and the final score is generally given as one of these categories rather than as a number or percentile ranking.

The Wechsler Intelligence Scales are standardized tests, meaning that as part of the test design, they were administered to a large representative sample of the target population, and norms were determined from the results. The scales have a mean, or average, standard score of 100 and a standard deviation of 15. The standard deviation indicates how far above or below the norm the subject's score is. For example, a ten-year-old is assessed with the WISC-III scale and achieves a full-scale IQ score of 85. The mean score of 100 is the average level at which all 10-year-olds in the representative sample performed. This child's score would be one standard deviation below that norm.

While the full-scale IQ score provides a reference point for evaluation, it is only an average of a variety of skill areas. A trained psychologist evaluates and interprets an child's performance on the scale's subtests to discover their strengths and weaknesses and offer recommendations based upon these findings. The only known risk of the Wechsler intelligence tests is that the results are misused or are given undue weight.

Results of intelligence tests should not be considered a complete indication of a child's future path. They are most useful in determining children who may need special attention, either because of disability or because of giftedness. Parents should consider the possible consequences carefully if they are considering telling their child the outcome of this or any other intelligence test.

Wechsler Preschool and Primary Scale of Intelligence

The Wechsler Preschool and Primary Scale of Intelligence (WPPSI) is an intelligence test designed for children ages 2 years 6 months to 7 years 3 months developed by David Wechsler in 1967. It is a descendent of the earlier Wechsler Adult Intelligence Scale and the Wechsler Intelligence Scale for Children tests. Since its original publication, the WPPSI has been revised twice in 1989 and 2002 followed by the UK version in 2003. The current version, WPPSI–III, published by Pearson Assessment, is a revision of the WPPSI-R. It provides subtest and composite scores that represent intellectual functioning in verbal and performance cognitive domains, as well as providing a composite score that represents a child's general intellectual ability.

The original WPPSI was developed as an intelligence

measure for 4-6 : 6yr olds in response to an increasing need for the assessment of preschoolers. The WPPSI was divided into eleven subtests, all of which were retained in the revision in 1990. The WPPSI-R expanded the age range to 3–7 years 3 months and introduced a new subtest, Object Assembly. WPPSI-III incorporates a number of significant changes. Additional subtests have been designed to enhance the measurement of Fluid Reasoning these are; Matrix Reasoning, Picture Concepts and Word Reasoning. Measures of Processing Speed have also been taken from the WISC-III, adapted for use with younger children and included as new subtests (Coding & Symbol Search). The age range has not only been lowered to 2 years 6 months but it has also been divided into two bands: 2 years 6months - 3years 11 months and 4–7 years 3 months, this was done in recognition of the substantial changes in cognitive development that occur during early childhood.

The WPPSI–III is composed of 14 subtests.

- Block Design – While viewing a constructed model or a picture in a stimulus book, the child uses one– or two–colour blocks to re-create the design within a specified time limit.
- Information – For Picture Items, the child responds to a question by choosing a picture from four response options. For Verbal Items, the child answers questions that address a broad range of general knowledge topics.
- Matrix Reasoning – The child looks at an incomplete matrix and selects the missing portion from 4 or 5 response options.
- Vocabulary – For Picture Items, the child names pictures that are displayed in a stimulus book. For Verbal Items, the child gives definitions for words that the examiner reads aloud.

- Picture Concepts – The child is presented with two or three rows of pictures and chooses one picture from each row to form a group with a common characteristic.
- Symbol Search – The child scans a search group and indicates whether a target symbol matches any of the symbols in the search group.
- Word Reasoning – The child is asked to identify the common concept being described in a series of increasingly specific clues.
- Coding – The child copies symbols that are paired with simple geometric shapes. Using a key, the child draws each symbol in its corresponding shape.
- Comprehension – The child answers questions based on his or her understanding of general principles and social situations.
- Picture Completion – The child views a picture and then points to or names the important missing part.
- Similarities – The child is read an incomplete sentence containing two concepts that share a common characteristic. The child is asked to complete the sentence by providing a response that reflects the shared characteristic.
- Receptive Vocabulary – The child looks at a group of four pictures and points to the one the examiner names aloud.
- Object Assembly – The child is presented with the pieces of a puzzle in a standard arrangement and fits the pieces together to form a meaningful whole within 90 seconds.
- Picture Naming – The child names pictures that are displayed in a stimulus book.

The WPPSI–III provides Verbal and Performance IQ scores as well as a Full Scale IQ score. In addition, the Processing Speed Quotient (known as the Processing Speed Index on previous Wechsler scales) can be derived for children aged 4 –

7 years 3 months, and a General Language Composite can be determined for children in both age bands (2 years 6 months – 3 years 11 months & 4–7 years 3 months). Children in the 2 years 6 months – 3 years 11 months age band are administered only five of the subtests: Receptive Vocabulary, Block Design, Information, Object Assembly, and Picture Naming.

Quotient and Composite scores have a mean of 100 and a standard deviation of 15. Subtest scaled scores have a mean of 10 and a standard deviation of 3. For Quotient and Composite score:

Below 70 is Extremely Low,

70-79 is Borderline,

80-89 is Low Average,

90-109 is Average,

110-119 is High Average,

120-129 is Superior,

130+ is Very Superior.

This is true for all Wechsler Scales.

The WPPSI can be used in several ways, for example:

- As an assessment of general intellectual functioning.
- As part of an assessment to identify intellectual giftedness.
- To identify cognitive delay and learning difficulties.

The clinical utility of the WPPSI-III can be improved and a richer picture of general function achieved when combined with other assessments. For example, when paired with the Children's IQ Scale a measure of learning and IQ functioning in children or the WIAT-II a measure of academic achievement, information can be gained on both cognitive ability and academic achievement in young children.

Combinations such as these would potentially be of use in educational settings and inform educational interventions. A further potentially useful pairing includes the used of the Adaptive Behaviour Assessment System; this pairing can result in information on cognitive and adaptive functioning, both of which are required for a proper diagnosis of learning difficulties.

However, it is important to consider and recognize the limitations of using assessments. Some studies show that intelligence tests such as the WPPSI-III, especially for pre-K level, are unreliable and their results vary widely with various factors such as retesting, practice, test administrator, time and place.

There are claims that some commercially available materials improve results simply by eliminating negative factors through familiarization which in turn puts children at a comfortable frame of mind. The US standardization of the WPPSI-III included 1,700 children aged 2 years 6 months – 7 years 3 months. The reliability coefficients for the WPPSI-III US composite scales range from .89 to .95. The UK sample for the WPPSI-III was collected between 2002–2003 and contained 805 children in an attempt to accurately represent the most current UK population of children aged 2 years 6 months to 7 years 3 months according to the 2001 UK census data. The UK validation project was conducted at City University under the direction of Professor John Rust.

The WPPSI-III has been formally linked with the WIAT-II. The relationship between the WPPSI-III and the WPPSI-R, WISC-III, BSID-II, DAS, WIAT-II and CMS was also explored in order to evaluate the assessment's reliability. A number of special group studies were also carried out during standardization in order to improve the clinical utility of the tool. These studies included children with mental retardation, developmental delay, language disorders, motor impairment, ADHD and those classed as gifted.

Wechsler Intelligence Scale for Children

The Wechsler Intelligence Scale for Children (WISC), developed by David Wechsler, is an individually administered intelligence test for children between the ages of 6 and 16 inclusive that can be completed without reading or writing. The WISC takes 65-80 minutes to administer and generates an IQ score which represents a child's general intellectual ability.

The original WISC was an adaption of several of the subtests which made up the Wechsler–Bellevue Intelligence Scale but also featured several subtests designed specifically for it. The subtests were organised into Verbal and Performance scales, and provided scores for Verbal IQ (VIQ), Performance IQ (PIQ), and Full Scale IQ (FSIQ). A revised edition was published in 1974 as the WISC-R, featuring the same subtests however the age range was changed from 5-15 to 6-16. The third edition was published in 1991 and brought with it a new subtest as a measure of processing speed.

In addition to the traditional VIQ, PIQ, and FSIQ scores, four new index scores were introduced to represent more narrow domains of cognitive function: the Verbal Comprehension Index (VCI), the Perceptual Organization Index (POI), the Freedom from Distractibility Index (FDI), and the Processing Speed Index (PSI).

The current version, the WISC-IV, was produced in 2003 followed by the UK version in 2004. Each successive version has re-normed the test to compensate for the Flynn effect. Ensuring not only that the norms do not become outdated which is suggested to result in inflated scores on intelligence measures, but that they are representative of the current population.

Additional updates and refinements include changes to the questions to make them less biased against minorities and females, and updated materials to make them more useful in the administration of the test.

The WISC is one of a family of Wechsler intelligence scales. Subjects 16 and over are tested with the Wechsler Adult Intelligence Scale (WAIS), and children ages three to seven years, three months are tested with the Wechsler Preschool and Primary Scale of Intelligence (WPPSI).

There is some overlap between tests, with children aged 7 being able to complete the WPPSI or the WISC-IV, and children aged 16 being able to complete the WISC-IV or the WAIS. Different floor and ceiling effects can be achieved using the different tests, allowing for a greater understanding of the child's abilities or deficits.

This means that a 16 year old child who has mental retardation may be tested using the WISC-IV so that the clinician may see the floor of their knowledge (the lowest level).

The WISC-IV is divided into fifteen subtests, ten of which formed part of the previous WISC III. The five new subtests include three core tests: Picture Concepts, Letter-Number Sequencing, Matrix Reasoning and two supplemental tests: Cancellation and Word Reasoning. The supplemental subtests are used to accommodate children in certain rare cases, or to make up for spoiled results which may occur from interruptions or other circumstances. Testers are allowed no more than two substitutions in any FSIQ test, or no more than one per index.

A total of five composite scores can be derived with the WISC-IV. The WISC-IV generates a Full Scale IQ (FSIQ) which represents overall cognitive ability, the four other composite scores are Verbal Comprehension index (VCI), Perceptual Reasoning Index (PRI), Processing Speed Index (PSI) and Working IQ Index (WMI).

Each of the ten core subtests is given equal weighting towards full scale IQ. There are three subtests for both VCI and PRI, thus they are given 30% weighting each; in addition, PSI and WMI are given weighting for their two subtests each. The WISC-IV also produces seven process scores on three subtests: block design, cancellation and digit span.

These scores are intended to provide more detailed information on cognitive abilities that contribute to performance on the subtest. These scores do not contribute to the composite scores.

The VCI's subtests are as follows:

Vocabulary – Examinee is asked to define a provided word.

Similarities – Asking how two words are alike/similar.

Comprehension – Questions about social situations or common concepts.

Information (supplemental) – General knowledge questions.

Word reasoning (supplemental) – A task involving clues that lead to a specific word, each clue adds more information about the object/word/concept.

The Verbal Comprehension Index is an overall measure of verbal concept formation (the child's ability to verbally reason) and is influenced by knowledge learned from the environment.

The PRI's subtests are as follows:

- Block Design – Children put together red-and-white blocks in a pattern according to a displayed model. This is timed, and some of the more difficult puzzles award bonuses for speed.
- Picture Concepts – Children are provided with a series of pictures presented in rows (either two or three rows) and

asked to determine which pictures go together, one from each row.

- Matrix Reasoning – Children are shown an array of pictures with one missing square, and select the picture that fits the array from five options.
- Picture Completion (supplemental) – Children are shown artwork of common objects with a missing part, and asked to identify the missing part by pointing and/or naming.

The WMI's (formerly known as Freedom from Distractibility Index) subtests are as follows:

- Digit Span – Children are orally given sequences of numbers and asked to repeat them, either as heard or in reverse order.
- Letter-Number Sequencing – Children are provided a series of numbers and letters and asked to provide them back to the examiner in a predetermined order.
- Arithmetic (supplemental) – Orally administered arithmetic questions. Timed.

The PSI's subtests are as follows:

- Coding – Children under 8 mark rows of shapes with different lines according to a code, children over 8 transcribe a digit-symbol code. The task is time-limited with bonuses for speed.
- Symbol Search – Children are given rows of symbols and target symbols, and asked to mark whether or not the target symbols appear in each row.
- Cancellation (supplemental) – Children scan random and structured arrangements of pictures and marks specific target pictures within a limited amount of time.

The WISC-IV US standardization sample consisted of 2,200 children between the ages of 6 and 16 years 11 months and the UK consisted of 780. Both standardizations included special group samples including the following: children identified as gifted, children with mild or moderate mental retardation, children with learning disorders (reading, reading/writing, math, reading/writing/math), children with ADHD, children with expressive and mixed receptive-expressive language disorders children with autistic disorder, children with Asperger's syndrome, children with open or closed head injury, and children with motor impairment.

WISC-IV is also validated with measures of achievement, IQ, adaptive behaviour, emotional intelligence, and giftedness. Equivalency studies were also conducted within the Wechsler family of tests enabling comparisons between various Wechsler scores over the lifespan.

A number of concurrent studies were conducted to examine the scale's reliability and validity. Evidence of the convergent and discriminant validity of the WISC-IV is provided by correlational studies with the following instruments: WISC-III, WPPSI-III, WAIS-III, WASI, WIAT-II, CMS, GRS, BarOn EQ, and the ABAS-II. Evidence of construct validity was provided through a series of exploratory and confirmatory factor-analytic studies and mean comparisons using matched samples of clinical and nonclinical children.

The WISC is used not only as an intelligence test, but as a clinical tool. Many practitioners use it to diagnose attention-deficit hyperactivity disorder (ADHD) and learning disabilities, for example.

This is usually done through a process called pattern analysis, in which the various subtests' scores are compared to one another (ipsative scoring) and clusters of unusually low scores in relation to the others are searched for. David Wechsler himself suggested this in 1958.

However, the research does not show this to be a very

effective way to diagnose ADHD or learning disabilities.The vast majority of ADHD children do not display certain subscores substantially below others, and many children who display such patterns do not have ADHD.

Other patterns for children with learning disabilities show a similar lack of usefulness of the WISC as a diagnostic tool.

When diagnosing children, best practice suggests that a multi-test battery (i.e., multi-factored evaluation) should be used as learning problems, attention, and emotional difficulties can have similar symptoms, co-occur, or reciprocally influence each other.

For example, children with learning difficulties can become emotionally distraught and thus have concentration difficulties, begin to exhibit behavior problems, or both. Children with ADD or ADHD may show learning difficulties because of their attention problems or also have learning disorder or mental retardation (or have nothing else).

In short, while diagnosis of any childhood or adult difficulty should never be made based on IQ alone (or interview, physician examination, parent report, other test etc. for that matter) the cognitive ability test can help rule out, in conjunction with other tests and sources of information, other explanations for problems, uncover co-morbid problems, and be a rich source of information when properly analysed and care is taken to avoid relying simply on the single summary IQ score.

The empirical consensus is that the WISC is best used as a tool to evaluate intelligence and not to diagnose ADHD or learning disabled children. It can be used to show discrepancies between a child's intelligence and his/her performance at school (and it is this discrepancy that School Psychologists look for when using this test).

In a clinical setting, learning disabilities are generally

diagnosed through a comparison of intelligence scores and scores on an achievement test, such as the Woodcock Johnson III or Wechsler Individual Achievement Test II. If a child's achievement is below what would be expected given their level of intellectual functioning (as derived from an IQ test such as the WISC-IV), then a learning disability may be present.

Subsequently, the WISC can be used as part of an assessment battery to identify intellectual giftedness, learning difficulties, and cognitive strengths and weaknesses.

When combined with other measures such as the Adaptive Behaviour Assessment System-II and the Children's IQ Scale it's clinical utility can be enhanced. Combinations such as these provide information on cognitive and adaptive functioning, both of which are required for the proper diagnosis of learning difficulties and learning and IQ functioning resulting in a richer picture of a child's cognitive functioning.

The WISC-IV has also been co formed with the Wechsler Individual Achievement Test-II UK, a measure of academic achievement. This linkage provides information on both cognitive ability and academic achievement in children. Tests of intellectual functioning are used extensively in school settings to evaluate specific cognitive deficits that may contribute to low academic achievement, and to predict future academic achievement. Using the WISC-IV in such a manner provides information for educational intervention purposes, such as interventions that address learning difficulties and cognitive deficits.

The WISC-IV can also be used to assess a child's cognitive development, with respect to the child's chronological age. Using such comparisons with other sources of data, the WISC can contribute information concerning a child's developmental and psychological well-being.

Very high or very low scores may suggest contributing

factors for adjustment difficulties in social contexts that present problems in accepting such developmental diversity (or that cannot accommodate more than a certain level of high cognitive functioning.)

Wechsler Intelligence Scale for Children

The most common assessment instrument used by psychologists is the Wechsler Intelligence Scale for Children and will therefore be the one we look at. The Wechsler test is, essentially, a test of intelligence. It has been in use for over fifty years and has been revised numerous times to keep it up to date.

The test is divided into two sections with each section containing a number of subtests. The two broad sections of the test are the

- Verbal Scale
- Performance Scale

Successful completion of any item on any of the Verbal subtests requires a verbal response. On the Performance subtests, the person must do something in response to a question or task. When the entire test has been administered, the assessor calculates what is called a Composite Score, a score that takes into account both sections. Because it is a test of intelligence, the test scores obtained are called IQ scores and you will see the results stated in this format:

- Verbal Scale IQ
- Performance Scale IQ
- Full Scale IQ (the composite score)

The Full Scale score, according to the standard interpretation, indicates the level of a person's intelligence. A Full Scale score in the range of 90 to 110 is considered average; the person can be said to have average intelligence.

In addition to looking at the Full Scale score, the three scores, (verbal, performance and full scale) can be compared against one another.

What is expected in most people is that the three scores will cluster close enough together to indicate that the individual's verbal and performance skills are evenly developed.

When there is a large difference between the two subtest scores (verbal and performance), it may indicate learning problems.

This is as good a time as any to introduce the reader to some of the common terms used in assessment:

- Percentile scores
- Reading age scores
- Standard scores

Children are frequently referred for assessment after reading or maths tests have been administered to the entire class. The most common whole-class tests in use are the Drumcondra tests (reading) and the Micra T test (mathematics). A child's results in these tests are reported in what are called percentile scores. A percentile score indicates where a child stands in comparison to a sample of children in his or her own age, on a given task. A score at the 50th percentile on the Drumcondra test means that the child is well within the middle range.

Some tests yield what are called reading age scores. Reading age scores do not yield significant information, their use has been criticised and has been discouraged in the learning support teachers' written guidelines. A two-year difference in reading age in 5th class may not be terribly significant.

Standard scores are also frequently reported following

assessment. The average standard score is 100, which is at the 50th percentile, meaning the child's score isn't significantly different in that test than other, same-age children.

Standard scores must differ from one another by about fifteen points in order for the difference to be of any real significance. About two-thirds of all children have standard scores on a test that are between 85 and 115, that is, the 16th percentile and the 84th percentile. Scores in this range are not particularly noteworthy.

The following chart will be helpful in translating standard scores, scale scores, standard deviations, and percentile scores into understandable and meaningful information. Standard deviations tell us how much confidence we can place in a given score.

Any time a test is administered there will be a certain range of scores obtained that don't have any significance in the actual test results. In psychological assessment the usual standard deviation of significance is three points or more. So if a child measures 12 points on a test and 11 on another there is no real significance to this difference. Although an oversimplification it is helpful to consider the standard deviation in scores to determine whether or not a strength or weakness is actually present upon assessment.

The most useful scores to interpret for common sense purposes are therefore percentile scores. Most importantly, do not expect reading- or mathematics-age scores to be useful for educational planning or for reviewing the effectiveness of educational interventions. We will refer to percentiles again throughout this section.

The Verbal Scale, Performance Scale, and Full Scale scores are all Standard Scores. Previously it was stated that standard scores all have 100 as their average, with the range of average being from 90 to 110. About two-thirds of all children will score between 85 and 115 on these three scales and scores within this range are not highly significant.

At the risk of getting bogged down in too much information, it's worth having a more detailed look. For example, let's take a look at the Verbal Scale.

- Information: Factual knowledge, long-term IQ, recall.
- Similarities: Abstract reasoning, verbal categories and concepts.
- Arithmetic: Attention and concentration, numerical reasoning.
- Vocabulary: Language development, word knowledge, verbal fluency.
- Comprehension: Social and practical judgment, common sense.
- Digit Span: Short-term auditory IQ, concentration.

On the Performance Scale, the following subtests are administered and what they are trying to assess is indicated:

- Picture Completion: Alertness to detail, visual discrimination.
- Coding: Visual-motor coordination, speed, and concentration.
- Picture Arrangement: Planning, logical thinking, social knowledge.
- Block Design: Spatial analysis, abstract visual problem solving.
- Object Assembly: visual analysis and construction of objects.
- Symbol Search: Visual-motor quickness, concentration, persistence.
- Mazes: Fine motor coordination, planning, following directions.

An example will help illustrate the fine points of interpreting this test. Suppose Ankita is referred for an educational psychological assessment, having progressed through Stages One and Two.

The Wechsler test is administered and she obtains the following results (this is a crude example for illustrative purposes and the numbers are not meant to be accurate representations of what a real test profile would look like). Individual subtest scores range from a low of one to a high of nineteen.

Remember that differences of three points or less between them are not particularly significant. When the difference exceeds three points it may indicate a difficulty with the underlying brain processing tasks that were described above.

Verbal Scale	**Performance Scale**
Information 8	Picture Completion 9
Similarities 3	Coding 10
Arithmetic 9	Picture Arrangements 11
Vocabulary 9	Block Design 2
Comprehension 18	Object Assembly 9
Digit Span 9	Symbol Search 8
Mazes 14	

Using the conversion tables available in the Wechsler test manual, the results of these subtests yield the following scale scores:

Verbal Scale IQ 109

Performance Scale IQ 113

Full Scale IQ 110

Ankita is in the average range. But if we take a closer look at the individual subtest scores, something interesting comes into view. On two subtests that assess abstract thinking (Similarities and Block Design), Ankita's subtest scores are quite low. Subtest scores have an average of ten and there is little significance in a variation of three. However, Ankita's score of 2 on Block Design and 3 on Similarities indicates a real weakness in abstract thinking, verbally and non-verbally, despite her average intelligence. This weakness may well indicate learning problems.

These scores help us to compare a child's test results with those of other, same-age children. Let's see how Ankita compares with other girls her age by looking at the percentile scores that correspond to each of her scores above, as follows:

Verbal Scale		**Performance Scale**	
Scale Score	**Percentile**	**Scale Score**	**Percentile**
Information 8	25	Picture Compilation 9	37
Similarities 3	1	Coding 10	50
Arithmetic 9	27	Picture Arrangement 11	63
Vocabulary 9	27	Block Design 2	1
Comprehension 18	99	Object Assembly 9	37
Digit Span 9	37	Symbol Search 8	25
Mazes 14	91		

The results of all these subtests yield the following scale scores:

Scale	**Score**	**Percentile**
Verbal Scale IQ	109	73
Performance Scale IQ	113	81
Full Scale IQ	110	75

Taking a look at the percentile scores tells us more about how Ankita compares to children her own age.

Now, let's suppose that Ankita was initially referred because she was having considerable difficulty learning to read. It is important to note here that the assessor must take into account all the factors that might result in Ankita's difficulty, before drawing conclusions.

She may have had health problems which caused her to miss one-third of the school year over each of the past several years; what if her parents were members of the Travelling Community and moved her from school to school five times each year? What if, for the past two years she has had three different teachers, as a result of staff illness, and two of them had no teaching qualification? There may be personal issues (family bereavement etc) that may have relevance.

Any of these factors, and more, could be the real cause of Ankita's reading problems. The assessor will have to take everything into account and put it together in a way that makes sense to all.

It is only possible to make full sense of test scores if they are stated in full in the assessment written report. It is often the case that the psychologist will only report a range of scores, for example, "Verbal IQ: Average Range", "Performance IQ: Borderline Range" This sort of report writing can raise more questions than answers because sometimes the numbers are at the fringes of a range.

For example a score of 90 and a score of 109 are both within the 'Average' range but are both at the extreme range, with one Low Average and one High Average. Without stating the exact numbers, it is impossible to get an accurate picture of the child's level of abilities.

In such a case, the complete test data (the actual numbers themselves) must be saved – it will be a useful means to compare results if an assessment is re-administered sometime in the future.

Scale Scores

This brings us to the range of scale scores and what they represent. The Wechsler test is supposed to be a test of intelligence and for these purposes, the three scale scores that are calculated correspond to a range of intelligence 'category', from Gifted to Learning Disabled:

Scale Score IQ	**Intelligence Range/Special Ed Category**
130 and above	Exceptionally Able/Gifted
90-110	Average (not a special education category)
70-79	Borderline General Learning Disability
50-68	Mild General Learning Disability
35-49	Moderate General Learning Disability
Below 35	Severe/Profound General Learning Disability

You might wonder what happens to those children whose scale scores fall between 80-89. The short answer is that they are not generally eligible for special education services; if their reading of mathematic ability is below the 10th percentile they will be looked after by the learning support teacher. If not, they are deemed to be doing as well as other children and will not receive any specialist assistance.

As has been stated, observations are a helpful source of information but it must be remembered that all observations are subjective (liable to be distorted by hidden bias and differing levels of tolerance for learning differences and differences in behavioural skills).

In any assessment the sole reliance upon observation and teacher-made tests is inappropriate. Assessment instruments that generate quantifiabledata are a necessary part of the assessment process.

Wechsler Adult Intelligence Scale

The Wechsler Adult Intelligence Scale Intelligence Quotient tests are the primary clinical instruments used to measure adult and adolescent intelligence. The original WAIS was published in February 1955 by David Wechsler, as a revision of the Wechsler-Bellevue Intelligence Scale. The fourth edition of the test was released in 2008 by Pearson.

The Wechsler-Bellevue tests were innovative in the 1930s because they gathered tasks created for nonclinical purposes for administration as a "clinical test battery". Because the Wechsler tests included non-verbal items (known as performance scales) as well as verbal items for all test-takers, and because the 1960 form of Lewis Terman's Stanford-Binet Intelligence Scales was less carefully developed than previous versions, Form I of the WAIS surpassed the Stanford-Binet tests in popularity by the 1960s.

Wechsler defined intelligence as "... the global capacity of a person to act purposefully, to think rationally, and to deal effectively with his environment

WAIS This section requires expansion with:

WAIS vs. WAIS-R

The WAIS was initially created as a revision of the Wechsler-Bellevue Intelligence Scale (WBIS), which was a battery of tests published by Wechsler in 1939. The WBIS was composed of subtests that could be found in various other intelligence tests of the time, such as Robert Yerkes' army testing programme and the Binet-Simon scale. The WAIS was first released in February 1955 by David Wechsler

The WAIS-R, a revised form of the WAIS, was released in 1981 and consisted of six verbal and five performance subtests. The verbal tests were: Information, Comprehension, Arithmetic, Digit Span, Similarities, and Vocabulary. The Performance subtests were: Picture Arrangement, Picture Completion, Block Design, Object Assembly, and Digit Symbol. A verbal IQ, performance IQ and full scale IQ were obtained.

This revised edition did not provide new validity data, but used the data from the original WAIS; however new norms were provided, carefully stratified.

The WAIS-III, a subsequent revision of the WAIS and the WAIS-R, was released in 1997. It provided scores for Verbal IQ, Performance IQ, and Full Scale IQ, along with four secondary indices (Verbal Comprehension, Working IQ, Perceptual Organisation, and Processing Speed).

Verbal IQ (VIQ)Included seven tests and provided two subindexes; verbal comprehension and working IQ.

The Verbal comprehension index included the following tests:

- Information
- Similarities
- Vocabulary

The Working IQ index included:

- Arithmetic
- Digit Span
- Letter-Number Sequencing and Comprehension are not included in these indices, but are used as substitutions for spoiled subtests within the WMI and VCI, respectively

Performance IQ (PIQ)Included six tests and it also

provided two subindexes; perceptual organization and processing speed.

The Perceptual organization index included:

- Block Design
- Matrix Reasoning
- Picture Completion

The Processing speed index included:

- Digit Symbol-Coding
- Symbol Search
- Two tests; Picture Arrangement and Object Assembly were not included in the indexes. Object Assembly is not included in the PIQ.

The current version of the test, the WAIS-IV, which was released in 2008, is composed of 10 core subtests and five supplemental subtests, with the 10 core subtests comprising the Full Scale IQ. With the new WAIS-IV, the verbal/performance subscales from previous versions were removed and replaced by the index scores. The General Ability Index (GAI) was included, which consists of the Similarities, Vocabulary and Information subtests from the Verbal Comprehension Index and the Block Design, Matrix Reasoning and Visual Puzzles subtests from the Perceptual Reasoning Index. The GAI is clinically useful because it can be used as a measure of cognitive abilities that are less vulnerable to impairment.

There are four index scores representing major components of intelligence:

- Verbal Comprehension Index (VCI)
- Perceptual Reasoning Index (PRI)
- Working IQ Index (WMI)

- Processing Speed Index (PSI)

Two broad scores are also generated, which can be used to summarise general intellectual abilities:

- Full Scale IQ (FSIQ), based on the total combined performance of the VCI, PRI, WMI, and PSI
- General Ability Index (GAI), based only on the six subtests that comprise the VCI and PRI

The Verbal Comprehension Index includes four tests:

- Similarities: Abstract verbal reasoning (e.g., "In what way are an apple and a pear alike?")
- Vocabulary: The degree to which one has learned, been able to comprehend and verbally express vocabulary (e.g., "What is a guitar?"
- Information: Degree of general information acquired from culture (e.g., "Who is the president of Russia?")
- Comprehension [Supplemental]: Ability to deal with abstract social conventions, rules and expressions (e.g., "What does kill 2 birds with 1 stone metaphorically mean?")

The Perceptual Reasoning Index comprises five tests

- Block Design: Spatial perception, visual abstract processing and problem-solving
- Matrix Reasoning: Nonverbal abstract problem-solving, inductive reasoning, spatial reasoning
- Visual Puzzles: non-verbal reasoning
- Picture Completion [Supplemental]: Ability to quickly perceive visual details
- Figure Weights [Supplemental]: quantitative and analogical reasoning

The Working IQ Index is obtained from three tests:

- Digit span: attention, concentration, mental control (e.g., Repeat the numbers 1-2-3 in reverse sequence)
- Arithmetic: Concentration while manipulating mental mathematical problems (e.g., "How many 2 Rupees stamps can you buy for a hundered rupee?")
- Letter-Number Sequencing [Supplemental]: attention and working IQ (e.g., Repeat the sequence Q-1-B-3-J-2, but place the numbers in numerical order and then the letters in alphabetical order)

The Processing Speed Index includes three tests:

- Symbol Search: Visual perception, speed
- Coding: Visual-motor coordination, motor and mental speed
- Cancellation [Supplemental]: visual-perceptual speed

The WAIS-IV was standardized on a sample of 2,200 people in the United States ranging in age from 16 to 90. An extension of the standardization has been conducted with 688 Canadians in the same age range. The median Full Scale IQ is centered at 100, with a standard deviation of 15. In a normal distribution, the IQ range of one standard deviation above and below the mean (i.e, between 85 and 115) is where approximately 68% of all adults would fall. The WAIS-IV measure is appropriate for use with individuals aged 16–90 years. For individuals under 16 years, the Wechsler Intelligence Scale for Children (WISC, 6-16 yrs) and the Wechsler Preschool and Primary Scale of Intelligence (WPPSI, 2 1/2-7yrs, 3 mos) are used.

A short, four-subtest version of the WAIS-III battery has been released, allowing clinicians to form a validated estimate of verbal, performance and full scale IQ in a shorter amount of time. The Wechsler Abbreviated Scale of Intelligence

(WASI) uses vocabulary, similarities, block design and matrix reasoning subtests similar to those of the WAIS to provide an estimate of full scale IQ in approximately 30 minutes. Intelligence tests may also be utilised in populations with psychiatric illness or brain injury, in order to assess level of cognitive functioning, though some regard this use as controversial. Some neuropsychologists use the technique on people suffering brain damage as it leads to links with which part of the brain has been affected, or use specific subtests in order to get an idea of the extent of the brain damage. For example, digit span may be used to get a sense of attentional difficulties. Others employ the WAIS-R NI (Wechsler Adult Intelligence Scale-Revised as a Neuropsychological Instrument), another measure published by Harcourt. Each subtest score is tallied and calculated with respect to non-normal or brain-damaged norms. As the WAIS is developed for the average, non-injured individual, separate norms were developed for appropriate comparison among similar functioning individuals.

■ ■■

CHAPTER 5

Exercises to Improve IQ

Physical Exercises

There are many physical exercises you can do to help you to increase your brain power. However, exercise on its own won't create the huge effects in intelligence that you want, if you also don't modify your behaviour and thinking.

So, using exercise is good, but just make sure that you also have other things in place to take advantage of the new found IQ that exercise is going to give you. Here are some helpful tips to successfully implement this part within your overall brain training programme:

- Physical exercise is an excellent way to improve the overall function of nervous system and brain.

  Not only does a better circulatory system lead to increased blood flow to the brain, but it also leads to a widening of the arteries which provide blood to it. The effects of this is that artery widening through carbon dioxide flow is permanent, so your brain will be able to take on new resources permanently through exercise. With more oxygen flowing to the brain, you are in a better position to operate your mind at its highest level.

- Train towards a particular goal.

  There is no point doing physical exercise, if you don't have a specific goal in mind which you want to accomplish. Have a specific goal which you want to achieve, and then follow through with that, by using various methods, is exactly what you need to make the most from it. Once the goal is set, create a training programme to achieve it. Make a list of steps, and then follow those steps to completion. This might be difficult at first, but it will become easier over time.

- Focus on physical exercises and sports one like and which will get one's heart pumping.

  The variety of things you can use here are extremely diverse. You can choose anything from athletics to team sports to solo running to swimming. Each training exercise will have unique benefits, but it can assist to enhance spatial intelligence, perception, hand to eye movement co-ordination, your ability to be precise, IQ abilities, mental alertness and lots of other things. The sports which you should really concentrate on are those that deal with heavy cardiovascular training, like running, swimming, rowing or cycling. You don't want to do things which are violent (e.g. rugby, boxing etc.) as the chance of injury is high. Stick to safe sports for your brain.

- Always try to be totally consistent in training schedule.

  The goal most certainly is not to win the Olympics. The objective is to use exercises to improve the health of your brain. The exercise you use isn't as important as maintaining consistency of the training to get solid results.

  After a while, you won't need to train at all, because the

permanent structual changes in your body which you are looking for will have taken place.

A good programme is one that is maintained for at least 6 months, but the longer the time spent, the better it will be. Longer training times means more time to allow your arteries to permanently widen, and this is vital for enhancing your mental functioning to much higher levels than previously.

Mental Exercises

The benefits of mental exercises are:

The benefits of physical fitness are obvious and visual. But, the benefits of mental fitness are even more important, although they might be more subtle. Here's just a few benefits:

- *Rapid learning*: Some people barely study for exams. Yet they manage to score good. It's because they learn quickly with an obejctive in mind.
- *Logical thinking*: Thinking logically will help you present things logically as well, which further will result in successful accomplishment of tasks.
- *Creativity*: Try to do simple tasks creatively. Or rather say, think of creative solutions for problems that might otherwise seem impossible to handle. You might not succeed at first, but results would soon follow.
- *Focus*: Start meditating to improve focus. At first, meditation might seem hard. It would appear impossible to control a visual scene or keep out distracting thoughts.

  But, over time, you'll notice huge improvements. You'll see yourself capable of holding images, ideas or focal points even with a fair degree of distraction.

There are two major ways to construct a mental fitness routine:

- Balancing projects/activities to ensure all mental 'muscles' are being worked intensely.
- Setting aside time to hit the mental gym with activities solely for the purpose of building brainpower.

  Here are some ideas for starting a mental fitness routine. Don't try to implement them all. Instead either set aside fifteen minutes a day for one of these or integrate one of them into your routine.

- Journaling – Writing down your thoughts is a great tool for problem solving.
- Meditation – There are serious uses for meditation in mental regimen. It is more spiritual than practical activity. Here are different meditations to work different mental muscles:
- Visualisation – Visualize a white apple and hold it in your mind. Then imagine yourself eating it a bite at a time. Experience all the sensations of touch, taste, sound, smell and sight. The hard part is keeping the mental image of your apple consistent with where and how you eat it. You can usually only go about 10 bites before the mental image degrades.
- Focused Breathing – Start by slowing your breathing to about 10-15 seconds per breath. Next focus on one specific part of your body on the inhale. Select a new focus on the exhale. You can then move this to noticing specific sounds or senses. A good exercise in focus.
- Self-Dialog – Meditation makes it easier to talk with yourself. You can invent characters that can dialog with you, helping explore ideas. Journaling is an easier form of introspection than meditation, but they both have their strengths.

- Cycle Hobbies – Take up new activities regularly. This will keep your learning curve steep so your mind is always engaged at a high intensity. You can go for painting, dancing, speaking, running, music, woodworking, programming, design and many others.
- Peripheral Activities – Don't just take new hobbies, take ones that are vastly different from each other. Being a mile wide doesn't just improve mental fitness, it gives you a broad base of metaphors for creativity.
- Read One Book Per Week – Make it a goal to read one book each week. Sometimes this can be difficult with time constraints, but the benefits are impressive. If you want to save time on this one, learn speed reading.
- Engaging Fiction – Engage yourself in movies, books or television that makes you think. Television that makes you think might sound like an oxymoron, but the medium isn't all bad if you know where to look. Engaging doesn't just mean entertaining, but that it actively challenges your assumptions.
- Puzzles – Solitary game playing can keep your mind sharp as long as the learning curve is steep and it doesn't become routine.
- Competitive Games – Games that require strategic thinking are excellent ways to boost your logic and empathizing skills. Chess may be an intellectual favourite, but newer games can hold more promise by being much more diverse, and having a deeper range of strategic options.
- Explore Another's Perspective – Empathy is a mental, not just an emotional, ability. Exploring another's perspective hones your ability to think through another's eyes. Although empathy is often dismissed as being touchy-feely and not logical, the ability to think from another's

perspective is an advanced mental ability that doesn't develop until we are several years old.

- Create Regularly – Always have a project on the go. After finishing your latest task, think about a new challenge.
- Thought Experiments – Einstein was famous for thought experiments. This kind of reasoning ability is a mark of intelligence. Ask yourself, "What if?"
- Break Routines – Try consciously breaking one of your habits, just for a moment. Eat a different breakfast. Take a different route to work. Sleep in the opposite direction.
- New Cultures – Expose yourself to different worldviews. Go to public gatherings and meet people from vastly different cultures to have a big effect on your ideas.
- Learn Outside Your Interests – Don't stick to what you like. Go for classes for things you don't know how to do.... cooking, craft, dancing, learning another language.... it can be anything.
- Friendly Debate – Discuss, don't argue. When you are in a debate you should try to persuade, but welcome opposing ideas not as attacks but opportunities. Debating forces you to examine your opinions.
- Teach – When you teach something, you'll often be surprised at how much better you understood the material through teaching it. Further, writing articles about you subject of expetise will help you organise those ideas inside your head.
- Practice New Skills – Mastery may be useful, but it might not be as valuable to mental discipline as just getting the basics. Unless a skill is useful to you, try to learn different skills just to adequacy and then moving to something different. It can take six months to understand 80% of a subject and sixty years to understand 95%.

- Force Constraints – Try washing yourself with your eyes closed. Cooking without sauces. Reading upside down. Extra constraints make problems more challenging, ramping up the mental intensity required.
- Interlink – Holistic learning is about linking ideas together. Spend some time to explore a subject and ask yourself how the pieces fit into other information. This will organize your thinking and improve your understanding.
- Increase Mental Intensity – Force yourself to use your brain more. All these ideas are just specific implementations to increase the mental intensity you face. Focus, strategy, logic and creativity are just a few of the mental muscles you should be exercising more regularly.
- Count the words in a single paragraph. Could be in a book or magazine, or it could be this paragraph. Doesn't matter. Just count the words, and then cound them again to make sure you counted correctly. After one paragraph becomes easier, move on to counting all the words in two paragraphs. Then do the whole page. Use only your eyes and do not point with your finger.
- Count in your head backwardsf rom one hundred to one. Then count from one hundred to one, but this time count in threes, such as 100, 97, 94, 91, 88, etc.
- To think no thoughts for at least five minutes. This is pretty tough, but you can do it. Start at one minute if you have to, and move up from there. Do your best to reach the goal of five minutes without thinking a single thought. This can take time, but over time you will improve and your concentration will excel along with it.

Games Exercises

We all are fond of playing games online and offline. Games can be defined as an activity that is merely done for enjoyment or sometimes for educational purpose. However, many of the games such as soccer, rugby, baseball, chess, etc. are largely played to have competition between the players in order to decide the winner. The winner of the game is usually the one who utilises his mental and physical activity above par to win the game. Many people hardly find any time to play games which means their physical and mental ability will comparatively lower than a sportsman who stays fit and plays game regularly. Most games need physical and mental stimulation to be played effectively. As it is said that games require mental stimulation, it is evitable that it improves one IQ level.

One can find infinite numbers of popular games online and the list of games is simply endless. Games can be classified in different categories such as quiz, trivia games, online games and real life games. Real life games include a wide range of games. Tug of war is one of the most common, popular and widely played real life games. This game is also known as rope pulling. The game is played between two different teams or sometime between two individuals. Both the teams have to compete with each other using a rope which is the tug. The winner is declared when one of the two teams managed to pull the opponent team in such a manner that they cross the center point. This game requires high physical stimulation as well as mental strategy as the game need to be played with techniques to favour the players.

Charades is one of the guessing games, which is also widely enjoyed by people around the globe. This games is known by different names in different parts of the world, however, the most common name for the game is Charades or Charade. The game is as interesting as any other quiz games or online trivia games. Charades also improves IQ as it involves lot of mental exercise in form of guess works. The game is based on acting and guessing skills. As one person acts out a word or a phrase and the other participant needs to guess the correct answer by understanding the sign language done by his teammate.

Trivia games are also one of the most interesting games that are enjoyed by people from all age groups. These games are filled with general knowledge sort of questions which needs to be answered. Like many other games trivia game also helps in enhancing your IQ level. Other games that are improves our mental skills include online quiz games, word search games, word puzzles, image puzzle, suduko.

Chess is one famous board game which is played in almost every country of the world. It can also be played online. The game highly stimulates mental ability of the players. It requires lot of mind work. There are many other such games that are played which not only offer enjoyment but also enhance IQ level. Card games such as solitaire, hearts, piquet, bridge, etc are very exciting games that will make you think of different strategies to win the game.

TV Games are one of the best ways to play games and improve your IQ by staying at the comfort of your home. Unlike other outdoor game which improves your physical strength, TV Games helps in enhancing your mental abilities and also improves your thought process. Various TV games have various difficulty levels. The more time you spend to think about different ways to clear the level, the more mentally sound you become.

On the internet, you can find many online quizzes, trivia games. You can also find umpteen numbers of skill games can be found online, one of the prominent ones being strategy games such as Evony. This game can be played through your web browser. You can also choose multiplayer option to play with anyone across the globe. There are other strategy games that can be played by means of DVDs on your PC such as

SimCity and Age of Empires. Such games can improve your IQ considerably.

Brain Exercises

Brain exercises are a fun way to boost brain power, but they should test you and present a fresh new way of tackling problems. You can employ simple techniques to challenge your brain, like putting on your socks the opposite way you normally do or sit in a different chair at mealtime. If you utilise more than one of your senses to learn something, it is less difficult to retain that information because the brain is a mechanism which links one piece of information to another.

A fantastic way to begin is by subscribing to your daily newspaper. There is a variety of mental toggling from sports to classifieds to comics, and the games like crossword and Sudoku are excellent brain exercises. Boosting your brain power can also be accomplished with other types of brain exercises. Experiment with your IQ. Commit to IQ a record of items – be it a task list, inventory of your refrigerator, etc. Go back after a time and try to remember what was on that list. In order to make sure the exercise taxes your brain enough, the stuff on the list should be difficult to remember.

Envision a route and sketch a map. After coming back from each new adventure you take, mentally visualise the area and sketch it. Instead of using a calculator, use your brain to compute numbers. Put aside the tablet, writing utensils, and laptop and compute the riddle in your head – for more fun, do while walking to the corner! Dare to expand your flavour sensations. Some recipes contain many herbs and spices . . . can you taste them all? Pump up your cooking knowledge. There are many different ways to prepare a meal, so challenge yourself by taking a cooking class or learning a new technique.

Each sense that we have is controlled by a separate section

of the brain, and since cooking utilizes all the senses we are using various sections of our brain. Develop symbolic sentences. Pick a word and form the image of the word in your mind, then ponder what other words begin or end with the same letters, have the same amount of letters, can be made from the letters rearranged, etc. Be taught a second (or third) language. You can aroûse the brain by paying attention to the sounds of the different words and phrases. Feel the music.

Analyse music or find out how to play a musical instrument. Develop your hand-eye coordination. Adopt a hobby like crocheting or needle-point, creating artwork with brushes or markers, putting together puzzles – things that utilise fine-motor functions; let your senses awaken. Find a way to occupy as many senses as you can with one endeavour, like gardening.

Develop the athlete within – there are a a lot of different sports that require both physical strength and mental awareness, such as basketball or golf.

The world has been educated that you can avoid heart disease by doing heart-healthy things, and in the very near future they will understand that they can increase their brain power by doing brain exercises. Science has proven that conducting yourself in a brain-healthy manner works wonders to maintain your brain strength, and we are soon to see a new decade of people committing to a routine of brain exercises to keep their brain alive and well.

■ ■ ■

CHAPTER 6

Foods that Improve IQ

Instead of following treatments that are based on drugs in order to improve their IQ, people should pay more attention to the foods they are consuming, as these can enhance the mental processes, too. Following a diet to improve IQ is easier, because the foods do not have side effects and contraindication. Of course, a selection must be made, as not all the foods are proper for improving the brain functions.

First of all, a diet to improve IQ should be based on foods that contain high amounts of iron. Iron deficiency anemia represents one of the main causes of poor school performance. Learning, thinking and recalling the information are performed with difficulty when the iron levels are below the normal limits. Also, a low level of iron in the body determines concentration problems.

Women who are between 19 and 50 years old require a greater amount of iron than men of the same age do. As many studies have shown, the iron level is correlated to the IQ. In order to increase the iron level back to normal, people are advised to follow a diet to improve IQ that is based on whole grain cereals and breads, beef, dried apricots and raisins. When the diet does not supply the necessary amount of iron, it is better to take some supplements.

The fruits and vegetables must be part of the diet to improve IQ, too. These, along with the carbohydrates, contain significant amounts of vitamins and minerals. They stimulate the brain and improve the overall health condition. The blueberries, for example, contain important quantities of antioxidants that improve the immune system by fighting the free radicals. The action of the free radicals is enhanced by the environmental toxins, such as radiation and air pollution.

Other fruits and vegetables that should be part of the diet to improve IQ include cantaloupe, watermelon, potatoes, radishes, strawberries, kale and red cabbage. The fruits and the vegetables also act as energy boosters. This way, they can be used in the treatment of depression, which is the major cause of IQ loss.

People who follow a diet to improve IQ should also consider consuming fish, such as sardines. Omega-3 fats, which represent an important part of the brain cells' membranes, is found in fish. A part of the omega-3 fats, which are also known as alpha linolenic acids, is transformed by the body into DHA.

Do you forget names of people or you can't remember what you had studied? If it is so you are facing IQ problem. IQ is one of the biggest assets of anyone. In absence of good IQ, you go on losing many things in your life. Some foods play vital role in enhancing your IQ. Here are the lists of a few foods which can boost your IQ.

Minerals affect your IQ a lot. For example if you are unable to concentrate in your studies or class it can be said that you have iron deficiency. When you have iron deficiency, your thinking and reasoning rate becomes very slow and you are unable to understand many things and reply any question very late.

Your brain functions well only when it gets sufficient amount of oxygen but in absence of iron, oxygen supply to your brain becomes very slow hence you face so many IQ problems. Therefore you should eat iron rich foods such as oat flakes, almonds, liver, chicken, cooked spinach, kidney, faggots, cashew nuts, wheat germ, sea vegetables, pumpkins, tofu, soy-beans, steamed clams, egg yolks, broccoli, asparagus, parsley, dates, etc.

Sodium and potassium rich foods such as fish, avocado, banana, cantaloupe, tomatoes, soy-flour, potato chips etc. provide you brain energy. Magnesium rich foods such as beans, spinach, nuts, oysters, raw-broccoli, mustard greens, flax seeds, pumpkin seeds, cucumber, barley, brown rice, banana, artichokes, almonds etc are very essential for your brain to work properly. To increase your thinking process you should eat Calcium rich foods such as tofu, almonds, milk, turnip, chick peas, yogurt, cheese etc. In absence of Calcium you will lack alertness and sharp or long lasting IQ.

Gingko biloba is an herb very useful for alertness and long term IQ. Due to it there is sufficient flow of oxygen to your brain. If you have weak IQ and can't concentrate in class, you can also use the root of Rhodiola rosea. To keep your brain and IQ functioning well you must drink plenty of water because our body is 70% water and ¾ of brain is water. If you don't drink sufficient water it will cause dehydration and thus your IQ power will decrease. For sharpness and concentration of your IQ you need to drink plenty of water.

IQ can easily be enhanced by ingesting certain types of natural foods. Cranberries have been proven to enhance IQ. Several tests have been done to prove this, and it is heavily suggested that women who were victims of rape involving the date rape drug could remember more about the assault and the offender if they had cranberry juice to drink beforehand.

Drinking pure cranberry juice may help enhance IQ so much that you can score a high grade on your school exam if you drink it while you study as well as during the exam.

IQ improve brain function by taking fish oil. You can eat fish, or you can simply take fish oil supplements that contain omega 3 6 9. Fish oil has long been proven to improve brain function, improve focus, improve concentration, and enhance IQ. Eating lots of fish or taking fish oil capsules will greatly improve IQ if it is part of your regular diet. Since this is a natural approach to improve IQ, it won't work instantly so you should not expect your IQ to improve right after taking a fish oil capsule. Your brain needs time to repair and rebuild your IQ so you'll need to incorporate foods that improve IQ as part of your regular diet and not just whenever you need a quick IQ boost. Other foods that are rich in protein such as nuts or meats, such as turkey, can also improve brain function therefore enhancing your IQ.

Peppermints have also long been proven to enhance IQ, so while you write your exam and while you study you should have some peppermints or even drink peppermint tea to exercise IQ. Aside from ingesting peppermints you can simply smell peppermint while studying and smell it again while writing your exam. Since peppermint does improve IQ, and scent is most closely tied in with your IQ in the brain, smelling peppermint can really improve IQ. Get some peppermint scented lotion, chapstick, or body spray to improve focus, improve concentration, enhance IQ, and exercise IQ.

In conclusion, eating foods such as fish, or taking fish oil capsules, a regular diet of protein-rich foods, drinking cranberry juice, and eating or smelling peppermints can really improve IQ.

Further, brain food fuels an optimum running brain. Balancing nutrients and exercise beats brain fog and helps maintain healthy long term health of your central nervous system.

The brain's main source of fuel is glucose. Glucose is an end product of carbohydrate metabolism which is used by brain cells for energy. Increased energy can result in improving IQ and mind power.

Unrefined complex carbohydrates such as whole grain products, carrots and legumes are excellent brain food choices. Their conversion to glucose takes place gradually ensuring a constant supply of energy. It's very important to balance starchy foods with lighter, green vegetables which supply blood-building minerals, powerful antioxidants and other health promoting properties.

Refined carbohydrates such as white sugar, white flour and white rice should be avoided. They are converted into glucose rapidly resulting in excessive blood sugar levels. The liver is forced to speed up glucose metabolism until blood sugar levels drop. Although refined sugar gives the body quick spurts of energy they tend to produce a 'yo-yo' effect in the blood sugar levels resulting in mood swings, disrupted attention spans and inability to concentrate.

Another reason to choose whole grains rather than their refined counterparts is the full range of amino acids, vitamins and minerals found in the outer layers of the grain. The milling process removes these nutrients.

Amino acids are the building blocks of protein in the body and essential for the production of neurotransmitters, the chemicals involved in the transmission of nerve impulses. Foods rich in amino acids promote mental alertness and increased energy levels. These should be consumed regularly throughout the day. Good sources of amino acids are also found in organic meats, eggs, nuts and seeds.

Vitamins and Minerals are Brain Food

B-complex vitamins are high on the list of helping to improve brain function. They're also essential for the proper synthesis of many other nutrients to help protect the integrity of the central nervous system. According to the FDA, a deficiency of B1 has been proven to be associated with IQ loss.

Niacin (B3) improves circulation to the brain. Pyridoxine (B6) plays an important role in glucose and protein metabolism. Cyanocobalamin (B12) is required for the synthesis of DNA and helps to maintain a health myelin sheath which insulates nerve cells. Folic acid is vital for DNA and RNA synthesis, protein metabolism, healthy cell division and red blood cell formation.

Also important for boosting brain function is Vitamin E. It promotes blood circulation to the brain and other tissues. Vitamin E preserves the cellular DNA repair function and fights free radicals.

Vitamin C promotes tissue regeneration and strengthens blood vessels throughout the body.

Calcium, magnesium, phosphorus and manganese are all important for healthy neurotransmitter activity. Chromium assists in the regulation of blood sugar levels and iron is required for the transport of oxygen to the brain tissue.

Good food choices of easily assimilable minerals are deep green leafy vegetables and seaweeds such as kelp and dulse.

Essential Fatty Acids (EFA)

Healthy brain cells also depend on an adequate supply of EFAs in the diet. These nourish and protect membranes surrounding our brain cells. EFAs also play an important role in facilitating the transmission of nerve impulses.

Excellent dietary sources for EFAs include: ocean fish, fresh nuts and seeds, deep green leafy vegetables, cold-pressed unrefined vegetable oils, flax seed and hemp oil.

Eat More Fish

Omega 3 oils –Studies have shown that foods rich in Omega-3 fats (such as fatty fish) reduce the cell inflammation that triggers IQ decline. Fatty fish such as sardines and salmon are excellent sources of Omega-3 oils, thus boosting IQ. It's advisable to eat at least three servings of fish (especially fatty ones) per week. Even if you eat only one serving, you're improving your IQ.

Eat More Vegetables

- Dark leafy vegetables – Have at least a cup a day. You can cook or boil green leafy vegetables, but just be careful not to overcook as this can take away vitamins and nutrients. Shoot for at least a cup of dark green leafy vegetables daily. Choose romaine over iceberg lettuce. Again, the darker the greens, the better for you. Also, include leafy vegetables such as kale, collard greens, etc.
- Spinach – A recent study showed how when rats were fed spinach, it not only prevented IQ loss, but even reversed it. That's probably because of spinach's high content of folic acid which has been proven to help Alzheimer's disease and other IQ losses due to aging. By only eating half a cup of cooked spinach each day, you get in 2/3 of your daily folic acid requirement.
- Onions – Onions contain fisetin, a naturally occurring flavonoid, which stimulates pathways that improve long-term IQ. Because they contain anthocyanin and quercetin, red onions are even better than yellow and white onions (which also contain significant amounts of quercetin.)

Interestingly, onions have been used for centuries in India to enhance IQ.

Berries to Improve IQ

- Blueberries – Because blueberries contain a colourful IQ-boosting phytochemical known as anthocyanins, they're excellent. Besides anthocyanin, they have other phytochemicals that produce good brain functioning. What's more, eating blueberries on a regular basis can help protect against a range of other age-related diseases such as diabetes, heart disease, and cancer.
- Strawberries – Strawberries also contain fisetin, which stimulates pathways that improve long-term IQ.

Other Fruits and Vegetables

Besides strawberries and onions, other fruits and vegetables, such as tomatoes, oranges, apples, peaches, grapes, kiwifruit, and persimmons also contain fisetin which helps IQ

Coffee Addicts

Coffee isn't bad, which is good news if you need a shot of caffeine to jump start your day. According to recent studies, coffee can help you focus better. Of course, if you have a medical problem (such as high cholesterol or other concerns), then limit your caffeine allowance to plain brewed coffee or tea. In other words, don't drink unfiltered coffee that's used to make espressos, cappuccinos, and lattes. If in doubt, it's better to be safe and don't drink coffee at all.

Don't Smoke

Besides harming your body, smoking also affects your IQ. Smokers performed worse than non-smokers on recent tests given in British magazine.

Exercise Regularly

If you're worried about losing IQ capabilities, then take aerobic exercise classes which can help IQ skills, as well as coordination.

A calm mind is capable of full concentration and solid metacognition abilities. Both vigorous, regular exercising and relaxation techniques have been shown to stimulate the production of brain chemicals which promote calmness and mental clarity. Regular exercising is also very important in decreasing the amount of brain-tissue loss that is associated with aging.

The human brain is like an engine. High octane fuel, regular maintenance and a daily run will help to increase overall performance.

List of Foods for Improving IQ

Further, some foods boost brain power and function more than others. The 14 following 'superfoods' are excellent sources of nutrients which will nourish the brain and the body.

- Whole grains: Whole grain foods such as breads and cereal provide needed folate, which brings oxygen-rich blood to the brain, and contain vitamin B6 and thiamine. Whole grains can enhance IQ and focus. Whole grain foods also contribute to sustained energy levels by stabilizing blood sugar levels.
- Eggs: Eggs are rich in choline which helps boost IQ and concentration. Eggs are easy to cook and delicious for any meal or snacks. They are also an excellent source of protein and can contribute to energy levels.
- Nuts: Walnuts are excellent sources of omega-3 and omega-6 fatty acids as well as vitamins E and B6, which assist with equalizing the brain's serotonin levels. Almonds offer the

nutrient riboflavin which boosts IQ. Pecans are high in choline which encourages IQ and brain development. Cashews are rich sources of magnesium which facilitates providing more oxygen to the brain.

- Berries (including strawberries, blackberries and blueberries): The ellagic acid in blueberries protects brain cells from being damaged. Antioxidants are found in strawberries, and the anthocyanins found in blackberries can prevent degenerative brain diseases. Berries can improve IQ and cognitive skills and assist with communication between brain cells.
- Seeds: Seeds and nuts can improve mood and and brain function by providing thiamine, zinc, Vitamins A and E, and omega 3 and 6 fatty acids.
- Wild salmon: Wild salmon is one of the richest sources of omega-3 essential fatty acids. Omega-3 fatty acids are important for mood, IQ, and concentration.
- Avocados: Avocados contain mono-unsaturated fats which assists in blood flow. The brain requires healthy fats in order to maintain focus and concentration. Avocados are delicious added to salads, made into dips or added to sandwiches.
- Tomatoes: The lypocene in tomatoes offers up powerful antioxidants which prevents damage from free radicals. Free radicals are a possible factor in the development in brain diseases such as Alzheimer's and dementia. Tomatoes also offer vitamins A and C as well as potassium.
- Red cabbage: Red cabbage contains polyphenols, which are antioxidants that prevent the cells from being damaged from free radicals. Cabbage is delicious added to soups, or can be cooked as a vegetable side dish.
- Spinach: Spinach offers plenty of folate which empowers

IQ, offers anti-aging benefits and assists IQ and concentration. Spinach is easily added to salads, sandwiches or can be served as a side dish.

- Green tea: Green tea contains catechines and polyphenols, which help the brain to relax and stimulates dopamine levels. Green tea increases IQ and concentration and can help sustain concentration levels. Tea can be added to the diet as a hot or cold drink anytime of day.
- Bananas: Bananas are loaded with nutrients such as vitamin B6, potassium, and folic acid which increase serotonin levels and mood. Bananas are simple to add to the diet as snacks, on cereals or in smoothies.
- Dark chocolate: Dark chocolate, which contains at least 70% cocoa, offers powerful antioxidants and flavonoids which boost blood circulation in the brain. Increased blood flow enables better concentration, IQ and cognitive processes. Dark chocolate is an excellent dessert or dark chocolate powder can be added to smoothies.
- Dry beans: Vitamin B5, folic acid, and magnesium can be found in dry beans. Proper brain function depends upon a healthy supply of B vitamins. Beans are easy to cook into a healthy soup or eaten with other foods such as salads.
- Proteins: All the functions of the brain: IQ, thinking, problem solving, sending messages to the body, are biochemical processes. Brain cells communicate with each other and with the body by sending messengers called neurotransmitters. Like many molecules in the body neurotransmitters are made from amino acids that are found in food protein such as meat, fish, eggs, nuts, lentils and dairy products. Vitamins and minerals are needed to convert these amino acids into these specialized neurotransmitters.

- Water: Our bodies are composed of almost 70% water and water makes up over 80% of blood which transports nutrients to the brain and eliminates toxins. Your brain needs to be fully hydrated for maximum concentration and mental alertness.

- Fat: Not all fat is bad; the body requires essential fatty acids because the brain is made up of more than 60% fat. Nerve cells in the brain are covered with a fatty myelin sheath that is crucial in transmitting messages quickly. Omega 3 fatty acids are essential fatty acids for optimum performance of the brain. A lack of omega-3 in the diet can lead to depression, failing IQ, low concentration and focus, reduced learning capacity and even ADD and other mental disorders.

  Foods that are rich in omega-3 fats include oil fish such as salmon, sardines, trout, tuna, herring, mackerel and anchovies and plant foods such as flax and pumpkin seeds. All you need is to add fish to your diet twice a week.

- Vitamins & Minerals: Vitamins and minerals are essential for the functioning and growth of the brain. Vitamins A, C and E are powerful antioxidants that help to protect the brain and preserve IQ. The 'B' complex vitamins are also important for the brain and play a vital role in producing energy.

- Blueberries: Blueberries have been shown in numerous studies to do wonderful things for IQ and the brain in general. Old rats that were fed blueberries scored the same as young rats on IQ tests. Blueberries contain anthocyanin, a known IQ-boosting phytochemical. They also contain many other phytochemicals that may contribute to healthy brain function.

- Apples: Apples contain high levels of quercetin, an antioxidant that has been shown in recent studies to protect against Alzheimer's disease. Although it is also present in the flesh, the most quercetin is found in the skin. Red apples also contain anthocyanin in their skins.

- Spinach: One study found that feeding rats spinach prevented and even reversed IQ loss. This may be due in part to its high folic acid content, a nutrient that is believed to be protective against Alzheimer's disease and age-related IQ loss. Just a half-cup of cooked spinach provides two-thirds your daily requirement of folic acid.
- Onions: Red onions contain anthocyanin and quercetin. Yellow and white onions also contain good levels of quercetin. In India, where onions are an important staple, onions have been used as a folk remedy to boost IQ for centuries.
- Broccoli: Broccoli contains quercetin. It's also a good source of folic acid.
- Red Beets: Beets are a good source of anthocyanin and folic acid.
- Grapes: Red, purple, and black grapes all contain quercetin and anthocyanin. Red wine also contains good levels of these phytochemicals, but overindulging in red wine may negate the benefits so keeping consumption to one glass per day may be wise.
- Cherries: Another red food that is a good source of anthocyanin.
- Eggplant: Eggplant is a great source of anthocyanin. It also contains nasunin, an antioxidant that protects the lipids in brain cell membranes.
- Rosemary: Researchers have found that the carnosic acid in rosemary is neuroprotective and may play a role in the prevention of Alzheimer's disease and other neurodegenerative brain disorders. One study even found

that just the scent of rosemary improved the memories of office workers.

- Fish: Herring, salmon, tuna, mackerel, halibut, anchovies, sardines and other cold-water fish are your best source of Omega-3 fatty acids, the primary components of the brain, retina and other nerve tissue. Studies have shown that Omega-3 fatty acids boost energy, enhance learning ability, improve problem-solving skills, and boost IQ power and enhance communication between brain cells.
- Soy: Foods made from whole, organic soybeans like soy milk and tofu are rich in choline, lecithin and isoflavones. Choline has been proven to positively impact brain development in addition to slowing IQ loss, lecithin helps in preventing deposits of plaque in the brain, and isoflavones help improve cognitive function, category fluency, logical IQ, spatial cognition and IQ recall.
- Colourful and citrus fruits: Fill your platter with all the colours of the rainbow and a few more, and you're guaranteed to improve your brain power. Avocados are especially potent in increasing blood flow to the brain because of their mono-unsaturated fat content. Other beneficial fruits that have a positive impact on your brain and help you recall information quickly include cantaloupes, watermelon, tomatoes, plums, pineapples, oranges, apples, grapes, kiwifruits, peaches and cherries.
- Berries: Blueberries are known for improving motor skills and learning capacity while strawberries are rich in fisetin, a flavenoid that improves IQ recall. Elderberries, blackberries and raspberries have other brain power boosting benefits through their antioxidant content.
- Cruciferous and leafy green vegetables: Your mother had a good reason for forcing you to eat your broccoli. Cabbages, kale, turnips, Brussels sprouts, broccoli, collard

greens, cauliflowers, radishes, spinach, mustard green and water cress all help retain IQ. Other vegetables that are good in boosting brain power are onions, red peppers, lettuce, carrots, asparagus, okra, mushrooms, broccoli and sprouts.

- Nuts: Rich in Vitamins E and B6, folate, Omega-3 and Omega-6 fatty acids, and antioxidants, these small food items boost your brain power and improve your mood. The whole nutty family of cashews, almonds, walnuts, hazelnuts, peanuts, Brazil nuts and pecans brings some benefit to your brain.
- Seeds: Flaxseeds are a rich source of IQ-boosting Omega-3 fatty acids. Roasted pumpkin seeds contain relaxing tryptophan and dry sunflower seeds offer thiamine, a form of Vitamin B that improves IQ and cognitive functions.
- Whole grains: The best brain stimulating foods are like financial news and information, they help the mind grow. Grains like whole wheat, wheat germ and bran that contain a high percentage of folate. Oatmeal, brown rice, whole-grain breads and cereals, barley and popcorn boost your blood flow to the brain. Wholegrain breads and cereals contain Vitamin B6 while wheat germ is rich in IQ-improving thiamine.
- Pulses and beans: The brain is fueled by glucose, and as it does not produce its own, the supply has to be kept steady from other sources. Rich in antioxidants, iron and other nutrients, beans help stabilize blood sugar levels. Peas, lentils, green beans, lima beans, black beans, kidney beans, and a variety of legumes help energize the brain.
- Sage: Whether used as a herb in your food or taken as a supplement in the form of oils and tablets, this member of the mint family has been known to boost levels of the chemical that helps transmit messages to and from the brain.

Sage helps in the break down of the enzyme acetylcholine that is needed for the brain to function properly.

- Curry: This spicy Eastern delicacy is good for your brain because of a key ingredient, turmeric. The chemical curcumin which is abundant in turmeric helps remove plaque from the brain.
- Tea: This wonder beverage, when freshly brewed, has been proven to improve IQ and focus as well as combat mental fatigue. Green tea is your best bet to good relax mentally and keep your wits sharpened because of the catechines it contains. Black tea, while not as potent as green tea, also works well as a brain enhancer.
- Eggs: A rich source of Vitamin B and lecithin, eggs are good providers of EFAs (essential fatty acids) to the brain. The yolk is especially rich in choline, a basic building block of brain cells that helps improve IQ.
- Calcium-rich foods: Yogurt, cheese, milk and other foods rich in calcium help in improving the function of nerves. Studies have proved that tyrosine, the amino acid in yogurt, is responsible for the production of the neurotransmitters dopamine and noradrenalin. In short, yogurt helps improve alertness and IQ.
- Iron-rich foods: A deficiency in iron has been proven to be the most common cause for poor concentration, decreasing intelligence and slow thinking processes. Iron is essential to supplying the brain with the oxygen it needs to continue normal activity. Red meats and liver are the best sources of dietary iron.
- Carbohydrate-rich foods: When eaten without protein or fat, carbohydrates provide a soothing effect to the brain. The glucose from the carbs provides the fuel the brain needs to energize you. Avoid refined carbohydrates like white bread, pastries and pasta though, as they cause lethargy.

Instead, stick to starches and sugars in the form of grains, legumes, fruits and vegetables.

- Supplemental herbs: Gingko biloba is one well-known supplement that improves mental clarity, alertness and IQ. It stimulates blood flow to the brain by dilating blood vessels and increasing the supply of oxygen. It also destroys free radicals that are detrimental to brain cells. Others, though not as popular, are equally effective. Rhodiola rosea is a root that is used in the treatment of poor attention span, tiredness and decreased IQ capacity. Herbalgram helps renovate oxygen-deprived cells while Panax ginseng has IQ enhancing effects.
- Organic and plant oils: Get things moving in your brain with IQ-boosting essential fatty acids. These EFAs can be found in oils such as olive, walnut and flaxseed.
- Whole-Grain Cereal and Orange Juice: Start your day out right by eating whole grain cereal and drinking a glass of orange juice for breakfast; both are rich in folic acid (also known as folate), which has been shown to contribute to better IQ and faster information processing. For midday munching, you can get folate from foods like soybeans, green peas, broccoli, and lentils.
- Cauliflower and Peanuts: A recent study done by McLean Hospital, an affiliate of Harvard Medical School, suggests that taking a minimum of 500 mg of citicoline supplements a day can help boost mental energy and efficacy. Citicoline, a natural substance found in all living cells, can also be ingested via cauliflower and peanuts—both are sources of choline, which is converted to citicoline in the brain.
- Broccoli, Sprouts, and Spinach: When ordering your salad at lunchtime, be sure to include these veggies; a 25-year Harvard Medical School study of more than 13,000 women showed that participants who ate cruciferous and

leafy greens retained their IQ best. The more you eat of these vegetables, the better!

- Grapes, and Plums: In terms of fruit, berries have some of the highest concentrations of antioxidants. Plus, they're packed with anthocyanin, a phytochemical that may help reverse age-related IQ loss and protect against the breakdown of brain cells. Quercetin, another phytochemical, produces similarly beneficial results. Blueberries, red apples, and darker-coloured grapes (red, black, and purple) are superpowerful, as they contain both of these flavonoids.
- Salmon and Sardines: Numerous studies have revealed the IQ-boosting properties of omega-3 fatty acid and certain fish—namely salmon, mackerel, sardines, and herring—are full of omega-3s. Eating these kinds of fish at least once a week will keep you thinking younger—three years younger, to be precise (a study by Rush University Medical Center in Chicago found that men and women who ate fish at this frequency had IQ functions equivalent to a person three years their junior). Not a fan of fish? Consider taking fish-oil supplements instead.
- Black Grape for the Better Brain Activity: Berries of black grape or black grape juice increase the levels of dopamine hormone that sharpens the IQ and stimulates brain activity. Having a glass of juice in the morning and a cluster of mouth-watering berries for the evening dessert would make you handle whatever complex intellectual tasks.
- Spinach to Prevent IQ Problems: Spinach contains lutein and some other antioxidants protecting brain cells from destruction. Spinach omelet makes a wonderful brain-protective breakfast meal. Hard wheat pasta with spinach is a perfect option for the early dinner.
- Raisin to Activate the Brain: Raisins contain a barium

compound that activates the IQ and ensures the optimal body tone. It is a great idea to have it for lunch at work instead of chips and snacks.

- Black Currant: Black currant is a rich source of vitamin C known to make us think clearer and being vigorous.
- Pumpkin Seeds: 1/2 cup of pumpkin seeds makes an essential zinc portion that enhances the IQ and accelerates the activity of the brain.
- Liver: Liver is a good source of the B vitamins. These vitamins ensure our vitality as well as improve the IQ and reduce nervousness.
- Salmon: The healthy fats found in salmon are the same fats found in your brain. These omega-3 fatty acids are believed to be critical to the proper development and functioning of your brain. The "superstar" of these omega-3 fats is "DHA" (docosahexaenoic), which is found in rich abundance in fish such as salmon.
- Avocados (Butterfruit): Avocados can aid in healthy blood flow and may even help to lower blood pressure as well as play a role in preventing strokes. They are quite fatty but it's the good fat that's helpful to your body not harmful. A healthy Blood flow means fresh oxygen is constantly supplied to the brain which improves concentration and thinking power.
- Almonds (Badam): Like fatty fish, almonds are high in omega-3 fatty acids. They are also rich in antioxidants, including vitamin E. Antioxidants support healthy brain cell communication through the neurotransmitter pathways, and promote healthy blood circulation, especially throughout the vast network of tiny blood vessels of the brain, enabling you to stay focused, alert, and functioning at peak mental capacity.

- Sunflower Seeds: Nuts have been highly touted as a great way to get healthy fats into your diet, but many people forget that seeds fall into this category too.

  Sunflower seeds are a rich source of vitamin E, with around 30 grams (one ounce) providing 30% of your total daily intake. Vitamin E is one of the primary antioxidants that will help decrease the decline of IQ as you age, making it one nutrient you'll want to be sure to consume.

- Sweet potatoes (Shakarkand): Sweet potatoes are especially brain-nourishing. They are rich in vitamin B6 (necessary for manufacturing a certain kind of neurotransmitters), as well as carbohydrates (the only fuel source the brain uses) and antioxidant nutrients (vitamin C and beta-carotene).

- Kidney beans (Rajma): Kidney beans improve your cognitive function. One cup of cooked kidney beans contains almost 19% of the RDV (Recommended Daily Value) for the B-vitamin thiamin. Thiamin is critical for cognitive function because it is needed to synthesize choline.

  Kidney beans are rich in inositol (part of the B-complex vitamin family). Inositol may improve symptoms of depression and mood disorders.

- Cranberries: Animal studies suggest that cranberries protect brain cells from free-radical damage. Moreover, consumption of this tart fruit is associated with improvements in IQ, balance and coordination.

- Green tea or coffee: A few years ago, European researchers found that individuals diagnosed with Alzheimer's, consumed far less caffeine than individuals who did not develop the disease. The theory is that caffeine's stimulating effect increases activity in the brain, blocking the development of proteins associated with an increased risk of Alzheimer's. Both coffee and green teas are also rich in antioxidants. If you are not a coffee or tea drinker, try some of the new green tea flavours on the market. However, too much caffeine can make you dependent and make you nervous, irritable, or bring on headaches.

- Carrots: Carrots contain a good source of vitamin C, beta carotene, and the B vitamins, which slow down the signs of aging and have been linked to improved IQ and reasoning.
- Soy: Soy has the advantage of being packed with protein, which triggers neurotransmitters associated with IQ. Soy protein isolate, which consists of a concentrated form of protein extracted from soybeans, is a great source of protein that can be found in supplements, liquid or powder form.

The demands on us as individuals are high and the pressure to perform at our best is ever present. Success in professional and social situations comes easier to those who are able to focus, concentrate and learn information quickly. To be able to express our personality and sparkle in conversation, we must fluently and speedily recall the information we have learned. Not just in a rote fashion, but with the ability to pluck gems of loosely connected information from our mind, and to bring it all together in inspired flashes of inventive, creative, and witty conversation.

Having developed our skills to the highest level that our natural potential can reach, it would be sad to lose it all simply through neglect of keeping our brain and nervous system healthy.

There are herbs that can enhance powers of IQ and concentration. Including herbs in our daily regime is one way in which we can offer our body the required help to keep it healthier.

Here is a list of herbs that contain the qualities that we are looking for:

- **Ginkgo Blloba:** One herb that has gained a strong reputation for its influence on the brain, and especially on IQ, is ginkgo biloba. It is a tree, which has existed for millions of years, and which has been used since ancient times for its ability to improve IQ and concentration. Clinical studies have clearly shown that Ginkgo has the power to address cerebral insufficiency, which 'often affects an individual with absent mindedness, poor IQ, lack of concentration, decreased physical performance, etc. Ginkgo has also been found very effective in treating age-related IQ impairment.

  Ginkgo increases the rate at which information is transmitted at the nerve-cell level. Ginkgo increases circulation, especially the circulation in tiny blood vessels, such as those in the brain. It dilates blood vessels by releasing a vessel-relaxing factor. This characteristic is able to improve oxygen and nutrient delivery to the brain, and is one of the reasons that ginkgo has gained a reputation for increasing IQ.

  The leaves of the Ginkgo biloba tree, also known as lbe maidenhair tree, have been used for more than 5,000 years for medicinal-purposes. It's one of the most widely used herbal extracts in Europe, and has been approved by the German government to treat symptoms of ageing, including cognitive disorders.

  Ginkgo has been shown to have the following effects:

1. Improve overall cognitive function and sharpen mental focus.
2. Prevent and treat symptoms of dementia.
3. Slow the progression of Alzheimer's in its early stages,

and progressive decrease in symptoms of Alzheimer's disease.

4. Treat "cerebral insufficiency", a slow decline in mental function associated with ageing and characterized by such symptoms as impaired concentration and IQ, confusion, and mood disorders.

5. Ginkgo works primarily by increasing blood flow and, consequentially, the supply of oxygen and nutrients to the brain. As a potent antioxidant, ginkgo helps protect against cellular damage.

- **Siberian Ginseng:** Siberian ginseng is another quality herb that is beneficial to both the brain and the central nervous system. It is known as an "adaptogen" and serves to balance the internal organs. It has consistently demonstrated an ability to increase the sense of well-being in a variety of psychological disturbances, including depression, insomnia, hypochondrias and various neuroses.

  Ginseng not only has powerful antioxidant properties, it has also been found to increase circulation which is associated with improved oxygen delivery and increased energy, similar to the effects of ginkgo biloba.

- **St. John's Wort:** This is a herb that is rapidly becoming popular for its effects on mood and anxiety. Recent research indicates that St. John's wort may be acting by increasing levels of the "feel good" neurotransmitter called serotonin, which actually is "brain food". St. John's wort has been effectively used to control depression.

- **Brahmi (Bacopa monniera):** Brahmi was traditionally used to treat mental illness, including epilepsy. It can help strengthen IQ, elevate brain function, increase concentration and mental focus, enhance mood and reduce the effects of stress. In India, it has long been incorporated in hair oils for massage. It has been used to provide a cooling effect to the scalp and to relax the nerves.

Brahmi contains substances called bacosides, which are responsible for improving IQ and IQ-related functions by enhancing the efficiency of nerve impulse transmission. Bacosides work by repairing damage to worn-out neurons.

- **Bllberry:** Bilberry, long known for its ability to improve eyesight, can help brain function as well. By increasing circulation and blood flow, bilberry works in much the same way as ginkgo. Additionally, it's a potent antioxidant and can prevent free radical damage to the brain.
- **Ginger:** Has the ability to improve the circulation and to support the central nervous system. It acts as a catalyst herb for other herbs, which are more specific in addressing IQ and concentration. It helps them to do their work more effectively.
- **Gotu Kola:** This herb is suggested for improving thought clarity and IQ. It is also considered excellent for promoting a feeling of calm and stress relief. Medicine. Traditionally used as a nerve tonic and a general tonic in times of physical and mental exertion, it is also widely used to assist in pain relief of arthritis. In ayurvedic medicine, the herb is also used for ailments of the nerves and mind including epilepsy, schizophrenia and IQ loss. The Chinese value Gotu Kola more as a plant that increases longevity and brain capacity than for any other purpose.

  It is able to rebuild energy reserves and for this reason it is called 'food for the brain'. It increases mental and physical power. It combats stress and improves reflexes. Gotu Kola has an energizing effect on the cells of the brain and is also said to help prevent nervous breakdown. It can relieve high blood pressure, mental fatigue and senility and helps the body defend itself against various toxins. It contains vitamins A, G, and K and is high in magnesium.

Some sources indicate that massive doses of Gotu Kola can produce narcotic effects. The evidence for this effect is sketchy at best and is controversial. No toxic effects are listed and Gotu Kola is considered to be quite safe by nearly all herbalists.

- **Ho Shou Wu:** In traditional Chinese medicine, Ho Shou Wu is considered an excellent tonic herb, which supports and calms the nervous system. It is considered appropriate for increasing energy levels due to its nutritive actions.
- **Linden:** Linden flowers are often recommended for their soothing actions and ability to transform restlessness into productive concentration.
- **Rosemary:** It is an excellent antioxidant herb, which has traditionally been used to enhance and improve IQ capabilities. It is considered a very good brain 'tonic', and is recommended for addressing headaches, especially those of a nervous tension origin.
- **Kelp:** It is one of the very best sources available for minerals. Kelp supplies the body with many of the nutrients required by all body systems, including the brain. When adequate supplies of vitamins and minerals are available, the body can function at a better level, with mental clarity and better mental performance.
- **Betony:** It is considered to be a very good nervine herb, which offers relief from anxiety and tension. Betony is a cerebral relaxant, that helps to calm a stressful mind.
- **Peppermint:** It is a traditional herb that is always a topic of research studies. Peppermint is useful for tension-related headaches. It is also considered to be very helpful in promoting mental clarity.

- **Rehmannia:** This is often used as a tonic in traditional Chinese medicine to relieve nervousness and calm the heart. It is also believed to act preventively against senility.
- **Skullcap:** It is an excellent herb which offers relief from nervous irritability and tension. It is considered useful for reducing worry and anxiety, thus allowing for clearer and more precise thinking processes.

Flower Essences

Flower therapy is a method of treating various psychological and emotional imbalances to prevent their manifestation as physical illness. Flower therapies may be helpful in treating various types of mental disorder, including anxiety, depression and stress. One study on flower essences showed that the flower therapy was effective on nearly 90 per cent of subjects. Flower essences are thought to work by encouraging a more balanced emotional and mental state.

Herbs should be an integral part of a healthy diet and lifestyle plan, which also includes adequate exercise and relaxation techniques. This information is intended for educational purposes only and is not intended to diagnose, treat or cure.

■■■

CHAPTER 7

Techniques to Improve IQ

Enhancing Children's IQ

Many of us will do whatever we can to assist children achieve success both in the school and future life. Parents try hard to make their children smart and talented by sending them to best school and by creating highly conducive environment for emotional and physical growth. But, in spite of putting hard effort, most of us are not really satisfied with the progress we achieve. In many cases, parents try to measure the degree of their children's success with the grades or scores achieved in the classroom. Sometimes, parents also try to compare their children's score with their peers in the class. Experts believe that such comparisons could be wrong and counter-productive in the long run as intelligence or talent are those characters that cannot be created nor can one establish.

Recent research findings suggest us that it is possible to raise and improve intelligence in children and adults at least by some degrees, by adapting a series of techniques and tricks. IQ is of intellectual brightness when compared to your peers.

A standard IQ test measures your intelligence by applying certain guidelines and principles. Most of the standard IQ tests are used to measure the level or degree of intelligence of a child depending on the age bracket. Under normal circumstances, the average IQ of person is around 100 while anything less than a score of 70 is not satisfactory.

Raising or improving your child's IQ is a difficult game as it involves manipulating your child's brain functions with a series of revolutionary techniques and methods. Improving your child's IQ means streamlining your child's thought process to suit and match a stimulating growing environment. One of the best methods to enhance your child's IQ is to create a stimulating environment in your home. It is possible to create a mentally stimulating and encouraging ambience for your child. Here are some basic methods that you can use to set up a stimulating environment in your home:

- Use highly expressive facial gestures while talking to your child; this simple process will help create a highly stimulating environment for brain growth.
- Reading bed time stories is another idea that helps your child understand text, language and voice signals.

  Help your child to mingle with other children so that he or she understands the power of association as well as partnership.
- Sign language and mimicking actions will help your child to learn a number of techniques like facial recognition, anticipation, guessing, thinking, analysing and evaluating.
- Just be there with your child whenever there is a real need. Children need support from their parents while they are doing homework or indulging themselves in some extra-curricular activities like painting and drawing.

- Active children are happy children! Physical activity that includes sports and games will boost a spurt in blood flow to all sensitive parts of body like brain and nervous system. Fresh blood with plenty of oxygen will help improve their body enhance the power of concentration, attention and thinking. Physical activity in children can promote clear thinking, step up creativity, stimulate the brain power, enhance concentration and provide conditions that are conducive for raising IQ.
- Extended physical play sessions will also help their body develop fine motor and cognitive skills.
- Playing chess and music are two of the well-recognised activities that can help raise IQ to higher levels. Introduce music and rhythm early in your child's life and watch your child perform better in class as well as other field of activities.
- Play chess with your child for some time everyday; chess is just like mental gymnastics and this intricate game helps your child develop the immense power of concentration as well as thinking process.

Though some experts believe that IQ tests are not the real indicators to measure the intelligence and talents of children, they do provide some basic insights on how your child can perform in some areas of scholastics and academics. But, parents should be cautious enough not to just rely on improving IQ in their children; successful children are those wonderful kids, who are not only better in their IQ scores, but also strong in their emotional and life skills.

Improving IQ in your children is an intensive activity that needs considerable amount of efforts and personal time from you. Improving IQ also means inching forward very slowly in a calibrated manner, so that you will not be rushing things in a hasty manner. Just remember that intelligence, talent and brilliance are the cherished birth gifts of God and there is a limit to what you can achieve with your children. Good nutrition, sound sleep, ample exercises and an array of brain boosting activities will help your children improve their IQ levels to certain extent.

Games to Improve IQ

Story Telling

One way to remember the information you need to commit to long-term IQ is to make up a story that 'connects' the items or facts you need to remember, thus making them easier to recall. The idea here is that it's easier to remember more information when one fact or item connects to another.

While making up the story, create a strong mental image of what's happening. This helps to 'connect' the data to an image and better cement it in your long-term IQ.

It's fun to practice using this technique in a group. Practice by laying out 20 or more objects on the table and trying to remember them.

Each member of the group takes his or her turn to add to the story by including another object.

If the first three objects are an apple, a key and a mobile phone, here's how the story might start:

Person 1: In the orchard, ripe apples were falling from the trees.

Person 2: But the gate to the orchard was locked and John had brought the wrong key.

Person 3: So he called Sue from his mobile phone to see if she could help.

Once all the objects have been included in the story, remove them all from the room. See who can remember the most items. Now tell the story again as a group, taking it in turns. The group will probably be able to remember the whole story and so recall all the items.

Pexeso: Matching Pairs

Pexeso involves matching pairs of like cards or tiles from a large group, when one of each group is hidden.

You play Pexeso with a set of cards or tiles that includes pairs of picture or numbers. You can play using half a pack of standard playing cards – just remove 2 of the 4 suits, so you have just 2 aces, 2 kings, 2 queens and so on.

Start by laying out 24 of the cards, making sure the 24 cards consists of 12 matched pairs. Once face down, move the cards around so that you do not know where any single card is located.

Turn one card over at a time, take a look at the number or object, and then turn it face down again. Repeat this process until you turn over a card that matches a card you turned over earlier. Now find the card's 'mate' by remembering from earlier where it is located. As you find a matched pair, remove them from the group. The number of cards dwindles until all the pairs are matched.

Time yourself and see how you improve (get faster) each time you play.

As you get better, increase the number of cards you start with, moving from the original 24 to 30, then to 36, 42 and so on.

'Blind' Jigsaw Puzzles

Another fun and inexpensive way to give your concentration

and IQ a boost is the good old-fashioned jigsaw puzzle. Playing it 'blind' means without referring back to the picture on the box!

First, look at a picture of the completed puzzle. Give yourself a few minutes to commit it to IQ.

Next, mix up the pieces to the jigsaw puzzle.

Now, work to put it back together without looking at the picture of the completed puzzle again (until you are done).

Trivia Quizzes

A great way to improve how well you recall information is to play trivia quizzes. The trivia can be about anything – movies, history, even about your specific business.

Whilst you can easily purchase trivia quiz board games and books, you can also make up your own questions when you are playing in a group.

Each person submits a list of questions (and answers!) and then to 'quiz master' takes questions from each person's list in turn.

When you play with a new set of trivia questions, you rely on your recall of prior knowledge and experience to find the answers. If you play with the same questions in a few days or weeks later, you will also rely on IQ of playing the game last time. Both new questions and re-runs are good for building you IQ skills.

Techniques for Enhancing IQ

Use Mnemonics

Mnemonics are simple IQ-improving tools that help you connect everyday, easy-to-remember items and ideas to information you want to remember. Later, by recalling these everyday items, you can also recall what you wanted to remember.

There are many mnemonic techniques:

- The Number/Rhyme Technique – This allows you to remember ordered lists. Start with a standard word that rhymes with the number (we recommend 1 – Bun, 2 – Shoe, 3 – Tree, 4 – Door, 5 – Hive, 6 – Bricks, 7 – Heaven, 8 – Gate, 9 – Line, 10 – Hen). Then create an image that associates each with the thing you're trying to remember.
- The Number/Shape System – Here, create images that relate to the shape of each number, and connect those images to the items in your list.
- The Alphabet Technique – This works well for lists of more than 9 or 10 items (beyond 10, the previous techniques can get too difficult). With this system, instead of finding a word that rhymes with the number, you associate the things you want to remember with a particular letter of the alphabet, from A to Z. This is an efficient way to remember an ordered list of up to 26 items.
- The Journey System – In your mind, think about a familiar journey or trip. For example, you might go from your office to your home. Associate the things that you want to remember with each landmark on your journey. With a long enough, well-enough known journey, you can remember a lot of things!
- The Roman Room System (Loci Method) – This technique uses location to stimulate your IQ. Connect your list with items you see in a familiar room or location. You might find associations with things in your kitchen, in your office, or at a familiar grocery store.

Mind Mapping

Mind maps (also called concept maps or IQ maps) are an

effective way to link ideas and concepts in your brain, and then 'see' the connections firsthand. Mind mapping is a note-taking technique that records information in a way that shows you how various pieces of information fit together. There's a lot of truth in the saying "A picture speaks a thousand words", and mind maps create an easily-remembered "picture" of the information you're trying to remember.

This technique is very useful to summarize and combine information from a variety of sources. It also allows you to think about complex problems in an organised manner, and then present your findings in a way that shows the details as well as the big picture.

The mind map itself is a useful end product. However, the process of creating the map is just as helpful for your IQ. Fitting all the pieces together, and looking for the connections, forces you to really understand what you're studying – and it keeps you from trying to simply memorize.

Challenge your Brain

As with other parts of your body, your mind needs exercise. You can exercise your brain by using it in different ways, on a regular basis. Try the following:

- Learn a new skill or start a hobby – Find activities that build skills you don't normally use in your daily life. For example, if you work with numbers all day, develop your creative side with art classes or photography.
- Use visualization on a regular basis – Since much of IQ involves associating and recalling images, it's important to build this skill. Get plenty of practice with this!
- Keep active socially – When you communicate and interact with people, you have to be alert. This helps keep your brain strong and alive.

- Focus on the important things – You can't possibly remember everything, so make sure you give your brain important things to do – and don't overload it with "waste." The "garbage in, garbage out" philosophy works well here.

Tip

While it's important to develop a good IQ, remembering unnecessary things (such as tasks you need to do, or things you need to buy) is hard work. What's more, because these consume short-term IQ, they can diminish your ability to concentrate on other things. They can also leave you stressed, as you struggle to remember all of the things you have to do.

Write these things down on your to-do list! This way, you don't have to remember everything. And if your IQ fails, you know where to look for the information you need.

- Keep your brain active with IQ games and puzzles – Try Sudoku, chess, Scrabble, and Word Twist as well as trivia games, pair matching, and puzzles. These are popular ways to practice memorization while having fun. And explore brain-training sites like Lumosity as a way of pepping up your mind.

Key Points

Your IQ is a valuable asset that you should protect and develop. Even if you no longer have to memorise information for exams, the ability to remember quickly and accurately is always important.

Whether it's remembering the name of someone you met at a conference last month, or recalling the sales figure from last quarter, you must rely on your IQ. Learn and practice the above techniques to keep your mind healthy.

You have only one brain – so treat it well, give it lots of

exercise, and don't take it for granted. You never know when you'll need its skills to be at their best!

The Link and Story Methods

The Link Method is one of the easiest mnemonic techniques available. You use it by making simple associations between items in a list, linking them with a vivid image containing the items.

Taking the first image, create a connection between it and the next item (perhaps in your mind smashing them together, putting one on top of the other, or suchlike.) Then move on through the list linking each item with the next.

The Story Method is very similar, linking items together with a memorable story featuring them. The flow of the story and the strength of the images give you the cues for retrieval.

How to Use the Tools?

It is quite possible to remember lists of words using association only. However it is often best to fit the associations into a story: Otherwise by forgetting just one association you can lose the whole of the rest of the list. Given the fluid structure of this mnemonic (compared with the peg systems explained later in this section) it is important that the images stored in your mind are as vivid as possible. Where a word you want to remember does not trigger strong images, use a similar word that will remind you of that word.

You could do this with two approaches, the Link Method and the Story Method:

Remembering with the Link Method

This would rely on a series of images coding information:

- An AVON (Avon) lady knocking on a heavy oak DOoR (Dorset)

- The DOoR opening to show a beautiful SuMmER landscape with a SETting sun (Somerset)
- The setting sun shines down onto a field of CORN (Cornwall)
- The CORN is so dry it is beginning to WILT (Wiltshire)
- The WILTing stalks slowly droop onto the tail of the sleeping DEVil (Devon).
- On the DEVil's horn a woman has impaled a GLOSsy (Gloucestershire) HAM (Hampshire) when she hit him over the head with it
- Now the Devil feels SoRRY (Surrey) he bothered her.

Note that there need not be any reason or underlying plot to the sequence of images: only images and the links between images are important.

Remembering with the Story Method

Alternatively you could code this information by imaging the following story vividly:

An AVON lady is walking up a path towards a strange house. She is hot and sweating slightly in the heat of high SUMMER (Somerset). Beside the path someone has planted giant CORN in a WALL (Cornwall), but it's beginning to WILT (Wiltshire) in the heat. She knocks on the DOoR (Dorset), which is opened by the DEVil (Devon).

In the background she can see a kitchen in which a servant is smearing honey on a HAM (Hampshire), making it GLOSsy (Gloucestershire) and gleam in bright sunlight streaming in through a window. Panicked by seeing the Devil, the Avon lady screams 'SoRRY' (Surrey), and dashes back down the path.

Key Points

The Link Method is probably the most basic IQ technique, and is very easy to understand and use. It works by coding information to be remembered into images and then linking these images together

The story technique is very similar. It links these images together into a story. This helps to keep events in a logical order and can improve your ability to remember information if you forget the sequence of images.

Both techniques are very simple to learn. Unfortunately they are both slightly unreliable as it is easy to confuse the order of images or forget images from a sequence.

The Number/Rhyme Mnemonic

The Number/Rhyme technique is a very simple way of remembering lists in order.

It is an example of a peg system using – a system where information is 'pegged' to a known sequence (here the numbers one to ten) to create pegwords. By doing this you ensure that you do not forget any facts, as gaps in information are immediately obvious. It also makes remembering images easier as you always know part of the mnemonic images.

At a simple level you can use it to remember things such as a list of English Kings or American Presidents in their precise order. At a more advanced level it can be used, for example, to code lists of experiments to be recalled in a science exam.

How to Use the Tool?

The technique works by helping you to build up pictures in your mind, in which you represent numbers by things that rhyme with the number. You can then link these pictures to images of the things to be remembered.

The usual rhyming scheme is:

Bun	Shoe	Tree	Paw
Hive	Bricks	Heaven	Gate
Line	Hen		

If you find that these images do not attract you or stick in your mind, then change them for something more meaningful.

Link these images to ones representing the things to be remembered. Often, the sillier the compound image, the more effectively you will remember it.

For example, you could remember a list of ten Greek philosophers as:

1. Parmenides – a BUN topped with grated yellow PARMEsan cheese.
2. Heraclitus – a SHOE worn by HERACLes (Greek Hercules) glowing with a bright LIghT.
3. Empedocles – a TREE from which the M-shaped McDonalds arches hang hooking up a bicycle PEDal.
4. Democritus – a PAW print on the voting form of a DEMOCRaTic election.
5. Protagoras – a bee HIVE being hit by an atomic PROTon.
6. Socrates – BRICKS falling onto a SOCk (with a foot inside!) from a CRATe.
7. Plato – a plate with angel's wings flapping around a white cloud.
8. Aristotle – a GATE being jumped by a bewigged French ARISTOcrat carrying a botTLE.
9. Zeno – a LINE of ZEN Buddhists meditating.
10. Epicurus – a flying HEN carrying an EPIdemic's CURe.

Try either visualising these images as suggested, or if you do not like them, come up with images of your own. Once you have done this, try writing down the names of the philosophers on a piece of paper. You should be able to do this by thinking of the number, then the part of the image associated with the number, and then the whole image. Finally you can decode the image to give you the name of the philosopher. If the mnemonic has worked, you should not only recall the names of all the philosophers in the correct order, but should also be able to spot where you have left them out of the sequence. Try it – it's easier than it sounds.

You can use a peg system like this as a basis for knowledge in an entire area. The example above could form the basis for knowledge of ancient philosophy. You could now associate images representing the projects, systems and theories of each philosopher with the images coding the philosophers' names.

Key Points

The Number/Rhyme technique is a very effective method of remembering lists. It works by 'pegging' the things to be remembered to images rhyming with the numbers 0 – 9. By driving the associations with numbers you have a good starting point in reconstructing the images, you are aware if information is missing, and you can pick up and continue the sequence from anywhere within the list.

The Journey System

The journey method is a powerful, flexible and effective mnemonic based around the idea of remembering landmarks on a well-known journey. It combines the narrative flow of the Link Method and the structure and order of the Peg Systems into one very powerful system.

How to Use the Tool?

You use the Journey Method by associating information with landmarks on a journey that you know well. This could, for example, be your journey to work in the morning; the route you use to get to the front door when you get up; the route to visit your parents; or a tour around a holiday destination. Once you are familiar with the technique you may be able to create imaginary journeys that fix in your mind, and apply these.

To use this technique most effectively, it is often best to prepare the journey beforehand. In this way the landmarks are clear in your mind before you try to commit information to them. One of the ways of doing this is to write down all the landmarks that you can recall in order on a piece of paper. This allows you to fix these landmarks as the significant ones to be used in your mnemonic, separating them from others that you may notice as you get to know the route even better.

To remember a list of items, whether these are people, experiments, events or objects, all you need do is associate these things with the landmarks or stops on your journey.

This is an extremely effective method of remembering long lists of information. With a sufficiently long journey you could, for example, remember elements on the periodic table, lists of Kings and Presidents, geographical information, or the order of cards in a shuffled pack.

The system is extremely flexible: all you need do to remember many items is to remember a longer journey with more landmarks. To remember a short list, only use part of the route!

One advantage of this technique is that you can use it to work both backwards and forwards, and start anywhere within the route to retrieve information.

You can use the technique well with other mnemonics. This can be done either by building complex coding images at the stops on a journey, or by linking to other mnemonics at each stop. You could start other journeys at each landmark. Alternatively, you may use a peg system to organise lists of journeys, etc.

Example: You may, as a simple example, want to remember something mundane like this shopping list:

Coffee, salad, vegetables, bread, kitchen paper, fish, chicken breasts, pork chops, soup, fruit, bath tub cleaner.

You could associate this list with a journey to a supermarket. Mnemonic images could be:

1. Front door: spilt coffee grains on the doormat.
2. Rose bush in front garden: growing lettuce leaves and tomatoes around the roses.
3. Car: with potatoes, onions and cauliflower on the driver's seat.
4. End of the road: an arch of French bread over the road.
5. Past garage: with its sign wrapped in kitchen roll.
6. Under railway bridge: from which haddock and cod are dangling by their tails.
7. Traffic lights: chickens squawking and flapping on top of lights.
8. Past church: in front of which a pig is doing karate, breaking boards.
9. Under office block: with a soup slick underneath: my car tires send up jets of tomato soup as I drive through it.
10. Past car park: with apples and oranges tumbling from the toplevel.

11. Supermarket car park: a filthy bath tub is parked in the space next to my car!

Key Points

The journey method is a powerful, effective method of remembering lists of information, by imagining images and events at stops on a journey.

As the journeys used are distinct in location and form, one list remembered using this technique is easy to distinguish from other lists.

To use this technique you need to invest some time in preparing journeys clearly in your mind. This investment pays off many times over by the application of the technique.

How to... Remember People's Names

Using the Tools

Remembering people's names needs a slightly different approach from all the others explained so far in this section. The techniques used, though, are quite simple:

1. Face Association

Examine a person's face discreetly when you are introduced. Try to find an unusual feature, whether ears, hairline, forehead, eyebrows, eyes, nose, mouth, chin, complexion, etc.

Create an association between that characteristic, the face, and the name in your mind. The association may be to link the person with someone else you know with the same name. Alternatively it may be to associate a rhyme or image of the name with the person's face or defining feature.

2. Repetition

When you are introduced, ask for the person to repeat their

name. Use the name yourself as often as possible (without overdoing it!). If it is unusual, ask how it is spelled or where it is comes from, and if appropriate, exchange cards. Keep in mind that the more often you hear and see the name, the more likely it is to sink in.

Also, after you have left that person's company, review the name in your mind several times. If you are particularly keen you might decide to write it down and make notes.

Summary

The methods suggested for remembering names are fairly simple and obvious, but are useful. Association either with images of a name or with other people can really help. Repetition and review help to confirm your IQ.

An important thing to stress is practice, patience, and progressive improvement.

■ ■■

CHAPTER 8

Games for Improving IQ

Games for Toddlers

A toddler needs a little more than adult babble for entertainment. Just as we get bored with mundane talking, they do too. Challenging activity pushes us to do more, get more and think more. Similarly a toddler too needs to be kept occupied, by making him think and adapt to the situations around him. IQ games for toddlers are designed with the same motive. These games have inherent educational strategies of providing knowledge, making the receiver analyse, helping him apply with a task, then making him think and finally be able to reach to an answer. Variations of puzzles, jigsaws and picture games are good IQ games that help your child develop a focus at a younger age. As toddlers enjoy these games with their parents, it becomes a group activity, making your child learn a few social skills, before he starts pre-school. Let's see what are some of the best IQ games for kids.

Hide and Seek

We've all played hide and seek at one point or the other. The object of the game for adults is thinking out of the box and searching through all the predictable and unpredictable places for hidden players. However, for a toddler playing hide and seek is about object permanence. This means that your toddler learns to look for things even if they cannot be seen by the naked eye. Cover yourself in a sheet and give clues to your toddler by saying, "Where's mom? Or where's dad?". Wave out once in a while to encourage him to come and find you. Once he finds you, swap your roles so that the purpose is learned in the reverse way too.

Reading and Comprehension

Turning reading and comprehension into a IQ game for your child is very simple. It can be played anywhere and does not require any special toys. Pick up any children's book, which has a lot of pictures and is extremely colourful. Read aloud and flip through the pages describing the animals and objects in the pictures to your child. Point things out to your child and allow your toddler to respond to it. Let your toddler take time to turn the pages and recognise the pictures and objects all over again. Doing this activity repeatedly will help you child learn about his surroundings at a faster pace. In return, it will also encourage him to speak and grasp words easily.

Mimicking

Natural curiosity of a toddler becomes a parent's greatest advantage. Children become what they see and do the things that very regularly witness. So choose your actions carefully and help you child develop a better IQ. Pulling faces, a dance move and mimicking is not just fun, but also an excellent learning tool. The purpose of this IQ game for children is to build motor skills, imagination and social skills. Encourage your toddler to copy your moves by seeing them once. This will not just strengthen IQ but will make it absolutely entertaining activity.

Abstract Art

An untrained mind can create the greatest art, for it fears no judgments. And herein lies your scope to make your child's doodle worth a better IQ. Children love scribbling on walls and every other thing they find. Join your toddler in this madness and make him name the colours of every crayon he pick up and every object he draws. Choose only primary colours in the beginning to avoid confusion. This game will also bring about fine motor control and hone his motor skills and imagination.

Sorting Games

By the time your toddler gets a little older than a year, he will be able to differentiate between colours, shapes and sizes. At this time, playing sorting games is a great way of honing his skills and strengthening his IQ with repetitive tasks that are presented in different ways. Doing this activity over and over again is will sharpen his sorting and building skills.

To retain your child's interest, make IQ games for toddlers challenging and entertaining. The moment any game takes a tone of seriousness, it'll become a boring activity, never to be played ever again. Give your child small treats and rewards to encourage and motivate him. Hope these games make teaching as much fun for you, as the need to satisfy the humongous inquisitiveness is for a child.

Games for Kids

There are several games for children that have been developed to enhance their IQ and act as brain exercises. If one looks at the core of these games, they'll find that even though the games appear to be simple, they have at their base certain techniques by which not only IQ but analytical and thinking power is also enhanced. Let us see what some of these improve IQ games are.

Add to the Story

Have a group of kids sit in a circle. Then let one of them pick up a chit that has a starting of any story like 'Once upon a time there was a king and queen' or anything that is a little more difficult even. The first kid starts the story and then adds something to it. The next kid has to say what the first and the second kid said and then add his own sentence. The fourth kid has to repeat the first 3 and add his own line and so it continues till it reaches a point where someone forgets something and they are disqualified. The circle then continues from where the story was left off. It can go on till they no one can continue a story. This is one of the best IQ games for adults as well.

Card Games

There are several card games that can help to make great IQ games for kids! Try the simplest of them all – turn the cards over and ask the kid to find the pairs. They are allowed to turn only two cards at a time and then turn them back. The challenge is to remember the order of the cards and try to get the pairs as quickly as possible. It can be a similar pair of the number from the total of four. This is more fun when played by a single kid and works as one of the best IQ match games for kids.

There are some specialized card games that are developed for the purpose of improving IQ as well. One such game is the 'Not at Home' game. In this, a group of kids are dealt a similar number of cards and the aim of the game is to try and get the entire deck in your hands. So you start by arranging the group of four cards in the deck (hearts, club, spade and diamond). A person starts and asks any random person in the circle whether they have a specific card, if that person does, the card is passed and they get another chance and if the person doesn't have the card, he says 'not at home' and the den is passed on to him. As the game progresses, it becomes more and more confusing to understand who had which card. It requires a cool head and the ability to keep things in mind without muddling them up. This is one of those games that is great not only for the kids but also acts as one of the best IQ games for seniors.

IQ *vs* Game

There are some ways on how to improve IQ and concentration, these have been used in the form of IQ verse games for kids. This is especially used in their curriculum because it makes for a great way to help them learn. In fact, it is a technique that has often been adopted to teach kids verses from the bible. The way it works is that you take a popular verse or a summarized version of a lesson and divide it into parts. Then write those parts on different chits and hide them all around a room or conjoin as part of scavenger hunt clues. The kids have to find all the chits and then arrange the verses in order. This helps them keep things in mind.

There are certain other IQ games for kids that have been used for centuries, these include solving puzzles, IQ games with different items arranged on a tray and the kids having to recall them back after they've seen them for a minute, Chinese whispers and more.

Including any of these IQ games for kids in their curriculum makes for not only entertainment factors but also develops their IQ power. And this is something your kids won't shirk from at any time.

Games for Children

Using the IQ games for children is one of the helpful techniques to improve the IQ skills and concentration of your child. These games are full of fun and perfect not only for the children, but the adults also can enjoy them. They can be a perfect recreation and distractive activity. You can use playing cards, puzzles or toys for playing the IQ games. Some of the common IQ games for children are IQ test, concentration, Chinese whispers, word associations, mismatches and communication.

- You can play the concentration game using a deck of 52 playing cards. Match up the pairs by memorising the location of each card.
- The IQ test can be played with a single child or a number of children using a pen and a paper. Arrange a tray with a selection of 5-20 common objects such as pencil, key, spoon, button, coin, etc. Cover this tray with a cloth before you bring it in the room. Let the kids have a view of the objects for 1-2 minutes and then cover it again. Ask the children to write down the list of objects that they have seen. A child writing the longest list from his/her IQ is declared winner of the game. When you are playing individually, you can change the game by removing one object and asking the child to identify which object is removed.
- Chinese whispers is another interesting IQ game for children. The kids are asked to sit in a line or a circle, so that they can whisper to their neighbour and not able to hear any players further away. The first player is given a short phrase that he/she whispers to the neighbour in a low voice. The neighbour then passes the message through the whispers. The game continues until the message is announced by the last player. The message received by the last player is often quite different from the original message. This game has no objective and no winner. It offers a good exercise to judge the IQ, listening capacity and power of gossip.
- The word association is one of the interesting IQ games for children. The children are asked to sit in a circle. The first child starts by saying any sentence in the story. The next child repeats the sentence and adds some information to that sentence. In this way, the kids continue to remember

the previous sentences and build up a story with their additions. This game can be altered by working through the matching items or alphabets to the first letter to each child's name. This game not only improves the IQ, but also encourages the child to be creative in story-telling.

- Mismatches is a good game for a small group of children. The kids are divided into two teams. One team is out of room, while another team makes mismatches by changing the objects in that room. After 3 minutes, the second team is allowed to enter the room. They are given one minute to spot the mismatches. The points are given on the basis of identification of mismatches. The team having the highest score is declared the winner.
- Communication is the IQ game that can be played indoors as well as outdoors. It tests the listening and communicating skills of the child. The children are given a plastic container, filled with exactly the same Legos, blocks etc. They are allowed to sit back-to-back, one is caller and other is listener. The caller explains the listener about how to put together the pieces. The listener makes sure about what he/she has understood. Once all the pieces have been used, the caller and the listener compare the structures to confirm about their communication. This game can also be played with felt and felt board, or paper and pen.
- There are several online IQ games available. There are wonderful CDs and DVDs of 3-D graphics and compelling tales that can attract the attention of children.

IQ games for children offer an opportunity to exercise their brains and help to improve their IQ as well as their language and concentration skills.

Games for Adults

Almost all adults get settled in their lives both – financially and also from the career point of view. In the adult age, most of the people have a fixed routine and sometimes, life becomes monotonous because of this. IQ games for adults can serve two purposes – maintaining the thinking and memorising capacity in adults alive and sharpening it. They also provide fun and entertainment, which gives a much needed break from the regular routines. Let us discuss in brief the importance of IQ games for adults in the succeeding paragraphs.

IQ games are useful for adults of all age groups. Many adults are very concerned about their IQ development and enhancement of creativity as their age goes on increasing. IQ games for adults are designed in such a way that they will test the knowledge and past IQ of adults by fielding questions on different topics such as sports, fashion, accessories, politics, etc. The useful IQ games for adults can stimulate the process of thinking by the mind and prevent the diseases like Alzheimers in adults.

Another advantage of these IQ games for adults is that they can be played forming a group of your friends and young members of your family. The basic fact about IQ is that it does not develop and in turn goes on declining, if we do not take efforts to use it consistently. There are many games online which you can play for your own benefit. Given below are some of the best games for seniors.

Exciting Games for Adults

Computer games for adults such as Monster garden and word bubbles help you to increase your IQ strength. The best thing about the monster game is that it helps in raising the standards of your spatial IQ and it gets tougher and tougher as you go on clearing the levels. The picture card game is also useful in IQ development. In this game, you see the pictures first and then spread them in a haphazard way on the floor. Then, you have to pick up a particular card and then find the one which is matching to the picture by memorizing the matching pairs which you have already seen earlier. The crossword puzzles and games test your long term IQ which is very essential. Scrabble is one of the online games, which is actually a board game. However, you can also play this game with other people. Pictionary, Trivial Pursuit and Trivial Pursuit Pop Culture Edition are some other games for adults.

The games for adults which involve kids, can be very fun filled. In these games, the kids can question the adults about different topics and one of the members is supposed to write down the scores. Every correct answer should be given five marks and after every wrong answer two marks should be deducted from the total score. The number of questions should be substantial so that proper justice is done to all the participants. The participant who wins should be given a handsome prize so that he feels motivated and is focused about his future development. Solving simple as well as difficult mathematical problems, by accurately remembering the mathematical formulas and concepts. Some fun riddles are also considered as the best games for adults.

Games for Seniors

Forgetfulness is a part of old age and it is a sad fact. Statistics reports show around 75% of senior people are concerned about their IQ-related problems. Lapse of IQ is not a disease and it could be reduced to a certain extent by engaging in brain exercises and IQ games. The only solution to this problem is to constantly play IQ-related games, which would help to keep your brain fit. Seniors, like kids, would love to play games. Some of the popular games that many senior citizens play even today are card games, bingo, Scrabble and Uno.

An elderly adult who has a IQ problem could improve his IQ by challenging his mind with puzzles, reading, crossword and other games. If you have grandchildren at home, take time out to play games with them. This would not only keep you mentally fit but also would be a good stress buster.

It would be a wise idea to pursue one of the hobbies that require concentration. For instance, a game of chess or solving a puzzle would mean racking your brain. This would enable you to retain your IQ and enhance mental capabilities. Studies show that a cup of coffee would revive the IQ of the people who have crossed 65 years of age. There are also reports to prove the IQ of a senior adult would be the best in the morning and it wanes by evening.

One of the IQ games a senior could play is crossword puzzle. You can either play it solely or else you could ask one of your friends or your spouse to join you. The first and foremost thing you need to do while playing crossword is to fill the crossword, using the clues given.

You can always use a dictionary. The crossword puzzle is one of the IQ games that young and the old love to play. This game would not only enhance your vocabulary but also keeps you mentally alert.

The seniors of a residential area should meet at least once a week or once in two weeks for a small tea party or a lunch get together. One of the party games seniors could play is the "I am going on a trip....". In this game, several senior adults sit in a circle. One of them should begin the game by saying, "I am going on a trip to some place, for instance, California, and in my holdall I am taking a pair of pants and a shirt."

The second person would say, "I am going on a trip to California and in my holdall I am taking a pair of pants and a shirt, and a.... (Fill in the blank.)". Continue the game till it comes back to the first person. He has to tell the original line plus items added in the holdall. This game is fun and helps the seniors to improve their IQ.

You could ask the senior to take a look at one of their favourite rooms, for instance, their bedroom for a minute. Ask him to leave the room. You can switch the articles in the room and also remove a few items from the shelves or dressing table. Ask the senior to come inside again and ask him to find out what is missing or which items have been switched. It would take some time for them to find out the missing and the switched items. But it is a fun game to improve one's IQ.

The other games that help to improve the long-term and the short-term IQ of seniors are checkers, chess and monopoly. As one grows old one should take up various activities along with his senior friends. There are many activities for senior citizens to revitalize their IQ and also to have fun.

IQ games for the senior citizens would help them to improve their IQ, also alleviate loneliness and to an extent reduce their health problems. Many brain-related health problems such as Alzheimer's, dementia and anxiety could be controlled or reduced with IQ games.

■ ■ ■

CHAPTER 9

Yoga for Improving IQ

IQ is critical to our daily lives. IQ is the capacity to retain information about past events, and helps us plan future events. We should be aware of how our memories work, what changes occur in IQ over time, and how we can improve our memories as we get older. Fortunately, most changes in IQ are normal changes of the aging process, or may be caused by temporary or treatable problems.

It is important to understand that there are IQ problems in all age groups. Children and teenagers seem to forget everything they've just been told. Many adults are so busy and have so many distractions, they just don't have time to remember everything. Seniors are more likely to have difficulty remembering names, items on a list, or where they put things. In general, no one has a "perfect" IQ. Most of what happens around us is forgotten because there's no need to remember everything. We are bombarded with information all the time and the IQ processes only the information that we need to remember.

There are many yogic techniques that stimulate the brain and nervous system to improve IQ and concentration.

Dharana- or the practice of Concentration. Dharana affects and reduces the occupied mind. The mind is kept firm at one place instead of letting it wander here and there. This reduces strain on the mind. The mental strength increases. With such habitual concentration, the work is done effectively and efficiently. The daily practice of dharana reduces the wavering attitude of mind and a different kind of peace can be observed throughout the day. The sixth limb of yoga, is a state of focused attention used during asana.

In asana, using a drishti (gazing point), especially during balancing postures, improves mental concentration. Spine lengthening postures, the forward and back bending poses, activate the spinal column and stimulate the nervous system.

Yogic exercises are helpful in improving intelligence and reducing forgetfulness. Practice the following yogic exercises with the feeling that the IQ power is improving and forgetfulness is reducing. Also take a balanced diet and chew you food nicely, as it helps to improves IQ. Remember all the things done throughout the day in a chronological order. This exercise will also help improve IQ power.

Yoga Asana

Yoga asanas provide excellent strength, both physical and mental. Regular practice of these exercises develops the physical and mental capabilities, which improve the IQ power, grasping power and intelligence. Sarvangasana and Bhujangasana are the two main asana for improving IQ. Regular practice of these asanas cure all one's physical and mental related problems, and thereby improve the IQ power.

Sarvangasana

Regular practice of this asana supplies pure blood to the brain. It makes the pituitary and pineal glands healthy, and activates the brain. It increases the IQ power, grasping power and intelligence, especially among children. It activates the thyroid and pituitary glands, which result in height increase.

This is beneficial for increasing height as it activates the thyroid and pituitary glands. It cures tiredness, weakness and obesity in children. It makes the eyes, ears, nose and other organs healthy. It improves the digestive system, activates the intestines, liver and increases the digestive fire. It cures enlarged liver, swelling, hysteria, hydrosil, hernia and constipation.

Method

1. Lie down straight on your back. The legs should be together, join the hands to the sides and rest the palms on the ground.
2. Inhale and raise the legs at 30 degrees upwards, then 60 degrees and then 90 degrees. You can support the back while lifting the legs.

   If the legs cannot be kept straight at 90 degrees take them back at 120 degrees and rest the hands at the back. The elbows should rest on the ground. The eyes should be closed, or otherwise look at your toes. In the beginning it can be done for 2 minutes and then slowly increase the time up to half an hour.
3. While coming back, keep the legs straight and bend backwards slightly. Remove both the hands from the back and rest them straight on the ground.

   Now, press the floor with the palms and get up in the same position as you had lied down, first back and then the legs should be laid straight on the floor. The duration for Sarvangasan and Shavasan should be the same.

Caution: Avoid this asana in case of neck and back pain.

Bhujangasana

This rejuvenating asana is also beneficial for improving IQ power. It cures backache, sciatica pain, slip disc, cervical spondalitis and other spinal problems.

It strengthens the thyroid, para-thyroid glands. It is useful in case of asthma.

It strengthens the liver and is useful in case of loss of appetite, acidity, diabetes and other stomach related problems. It makes the backbone flexible and healthy.

Method

Lie down on your stomach; keep the palms on the ground on both sides of the chest. The elbows should be lifted upwards and the shoulders should be close to the chest.

The legs should be straight and joined together. The palms should be stretched facing the spine and resting on the ground. Inhale and raise the chest and head upwards. The area below the navel should rest on the ground. Raise the head and move the neck backwards as much as you can. Remain in this position for 30 seconds. Repeat as many times as you can.

Caution: Do not practice this asana in case of hernia.

Pranayama

Regular practice of pranayama along with asana is helpful for all round development and improvement of the IQ power.

Bhastrika, Kapalbhati and Brahmari Pranayama are the best for this. They improve the IQ power and cure forgetfulness. Please note that the descriptions below are summaries. Please look up the articles on the specific pranayama for detailed instructions.

Kapalbhati Pranayama

This pranayama supplies pure life energy to the brain. It increases the blood circulation in the brain and removes blood clots thereby improving the IQ power. Other than this, the toxic and foreign substances from the body are evacuated. It cures cold catarrh, sinusitis, allergy, tension and other diseases. It is very useful in cases of phlegm, skin disease, asthma, heart disease, high and low blood pressure, depression, tiredness, laziness, sleeplessness, migraine, joint pain, etc. Obesity, diabetes, constipation, indigestion, gastric problem, disinterest and other disease are cured and it gives vitality. As a result the whole body becomes healthy and disease free.

Method

Be seated in a comfortable posture. Padmasana (crossed leg) and Vajrasana are the ideal yoga postures to practice pranayama. Place your hands on your knees. Feel relaxed. Focus on your breathing pattern.

Take a deep breath in and then release the breath out. Now inhale slowly and exhale with a great force. Your abdominal muscles should get expanded when you inhale and get contracted when you exhale.

The exhalations should be forceful. This exercise is similar to that of blowing your nose. The process of inhalation and exhalation should be constant. Make sure that while exhaling, you are throwing the air out from the lungs with full force.

Do not take much effort while inhaling the air. Complete the procedure of Kapalbhati pranayama by deep inhalation and exhalation.

You have successfully completed one round of Kapalbhati pranayama. A learner can do 3 rounds of Kapalbhati pranayama by doing 15 exhalations in each round. Take small breaks between each round. You can increase the number of exhalations and rounds of pranayama as per your convenience.

Bhastrika Pranayama

Health improves when the brain gets pure life energy. The prana and mind become stable, nervous weakness is cured and IQ power improves. It cures the tridosha (vata, pitta, kapha) and problems arising from brain. This cures forgetfulness. It improves appetite. It is beneficial in case of low blood pressure, depression, sleeplessness, knee pain, cold catarrh, headache, diabetes, obesity, loss of appetite and asthma.

It cures thyroid and tonsils and other throat related diseases.

It strengthens the heart and lungs. It is helpful in case of arousal of kundalini and prana.

Method

Sit in Padmasana. Inhale with full strength and exhale from both the nostrils as strongly as you can. Repeat inhaling and exhaling. Rest when you are tired or exhale completely after practicing this for 30-40 times.

Now place the hand near the nose and close the left nostril. Breathe from right nostril. Breathe in as much as you can, put Jalandhar Bandh followed by Moolbandh. Stop the breathe for some time. Remove the bandh and exhale from left nostril. This is one cycle of Bhastrika Pranayam. Repeat two to three times.

Caution: Do not shake the body while inhaling and exhaling. Do not practice it in case of high blood pressure, piles, acidity of perspiration due to heat.

Brahmari Pranayama

It cures brain generated problems, tension, worries, anger, sleeplessness, depression and other problems and improves the IQ power. It cures anxiety and is useful in case of restlessness, high blood pressure, heart disease etc.

It cures diabetes, obesity, asthma, nervous weakness, and improve the IQ power.

It is beneficial in case of gynecological diseases. It cures vata, pitta, kapha and other problems. It is also beneficial in case of headache, cold catarrh, etc.

Method

Sit in Padmasana and exhale from the nostrils slowly. Then inhale slowly. Inhale as much as you can and while exhaling produce a nasal sound. As if you are trying to produce the ma sound while chanting Om or like the honeybee whirling around the flowers. Produce this sound and exhale. Try to make this sound as sweet as possible. Close the ears with the thumbs in order to block the external noises and keep the fingers on the forehead. Inhale and exhale and produce the sound. Repeat this exercise for five minutes.

Caution: Do not shake the body while inhaling and exhaling. Do not practice it in case of high blood pressure, piles, acidity or perspiration due to heat.

Omkar Chanting

Omkar chanting improves the IQ power. It increases the mental strengths. It arouses the Kundalini. It establishes contacts with the extraterrestrial powers.

Method

Omkar is very significant in our lives. The letters A, U and M collectively make this word. The joint powers of Brahma, Vishnu and Mahesh are included in this word. Om is powerful and spread in the entire universe but we cannot experience it. Om should be chanted for introspection, produce energy in the body and circulate the strength.

Inhale and chant A (ah), then close the mouth and say U (oo) and then close and say M (im).

Stressing on the letter A, U and M cures the diseases of stomach, chest and brain respectively.

It is useful for improving the IQ power.

Trataka

Trataka (which means steady gaze) is a technique whereby the eyes are fixed upon a certain external point such as the horizon of the sea, or the flame of a candle.

Trataka 1

- Take a comfortable seated position outdoors, where objects at various distances between you and the horizon can be viewed.
- Pick at least 4 objects (roughly spaced equal distance), the first being near the feet and the furthest at the horizon.
- Beginning at the nearest object, concentrate upon it for 60 seconds.
- Move you attention every 60-seconds to each successively further object until the final one at the horizon has been reached.
- After focusing upon the last point for 60 seconds, reverse object by object (again concentrating 60 seconds on each) back to the first point.

Trataka 2

- Place a candle upon a small table, whereby the flame is at eye-level.
- Sit a distance of between 6 to 10 feet away and place your concentration upon the flame.

- Do not to blink and try to hold you concentration for between 30 and 60 seconds.
- Close you eyes for 30 to 60 seconds and try to reproduce the image of the flame in your 'mind's eye'.
- Repeat this process 3 to 6 times in one sitting.

Nasarga Drishthi

- Take a comfortable sitting position and gaze open-eyed at the tip of the nose.
- Hold this concentration until you feel tension in the eyes, then
- Close your eyelids, but imagine that you are still gazing at the tip of the nose.
- Hold this visualisation for 15-20 seconds and then re-open the eyes.
- Repeat this process several times.

Bhrumadhya Drishthi

- Again, take a comfortable sitting position and turn the gaze to the base of the nose, creating a 'cross-eyed' position.
- Raise the eyes slightly, so that this cross-eyed gaze now falls directly between the eyebrows, then...
- Close your eyelids and hold this point of concentration 'inwardly'.
- Periodically open your eyes to see if this point is being maintained, then close them once again.
- Hold this concentration for several minutes.

Open-legged Forward Bend

1. Stand tall with your feet about 3 feet apart. Pivot on the

balls of your feet to turn your heels out slightly. Imagine you are squeezing a beach ball between your thighs throughout this pose; this will help you keep your balance. Lift your chest toward the ceiling and inhale.

2. Exhale as you slowly bend forward from your hips with a flat back until you can touch the floor with the palms of your hands, keeping them shoulder-width apart, as pictured. You may need to stack books on the floor in front of you and rest your hands on them. Inhale and lengthen your spine.
3. Exhale and lower your torso toward your knees. Look at the wall behind you. Bend your elbows to point toward that wall. If you're very flexible, you may be able to move your hands in line with your toes, and your head may touch the floor, as pictured. Otherwise, let your torso and head hang loosely. Press your shoulders away from your ears. Hold for 3 to 10 deep breaths.
4. To release, put your hands on your hips, press down into your feet, and maintain a flat back as you return to the standing position. Step your feet together and pause for several breaths.

Threading The Needle

1. Start in Table pose, with your hands directly under your shoulders and your knees directly under your hips.
2. Slide your left hand forward a few inches along the floor. Lift your right hand and turn it over so your palm faces up, and turn your fingertips to point to the left.
3. Imagine that your right arm is the thread: Slide your right arm along the floor as far as you can through the needle,

the space between your left hand and left knee. Lower your right ear and shoulder to the floor, as pictured. If this is too difficult, instead lower your right forearm to the floor and turn your head to look over your left shoulder. Take 3 to 10 breaths. Release any tension in the muscles you aren't using, especially your facial muscles.

4. If you want a more advanced stretch, lift your left arm straight overhead. Turn your head to the left to look up at it. Lower your left hand to the floor.
5. To release, press down into your left hand as you lift with your abdominal muscles to return to Table pose. Repeat steps 2 to 4 on the opposite side.

Dragon Breathing

1. Stand tall with your feet about hip-width apart. Take several deep breaths in and out through your nose. And then inhale fully through your nose.
2. As you exhale, bend your knees, place your hands on your thighs, and move your torso a few inches forward with a flat back. Open your mouth and make a loud "Haaa!" sound, as if you are a fierce dragon breathing fire, as pictured. The exhalation should start in your belly and continue until you feel that every little bit of stale air has left your body.
3. Return to a standing position as you inhale fully through your nose. Repeat step 2 five more times, inhaling fully each time you return to a standing position. When you're done, stand or sit quietly and allow your breathing to return to its natural rhythm.

The most important adjunct to IQ development in the

Causal Body (Anandamaya Kosa) is the wisdom of discrimination with understanding.

Furthermore, this should be at all points of time and under all circumstances in order to be in tune with all creation. For the highest souls the IQ of the Self is to such an extent that such a soul never looses aware ness of that bliss. It is a state of absolute expansiveness and delightful awareness, a state of internal silence. For this, one has to only be. The only means adopted at this level is what is called Self Enquiry: The repetitive questioning of "Who am I?"

Yoga therapy IQ development at Intellectual level (Vijnanamaya Kosa)

When the mind is flooded with inner light, dreams no longer exist. Then all that remains is bliss. The Yoga therapy method for IQ development at this stage is, first and foremost, hearing – or reading – about the higher and more comprehensive perspectives of God's creation. Then one gets down to analysing this through reasoning, with an open mind free of prejudices, disbelief or blind belief.

This is to be done just like true scientists experimenting through examination, intense search within. The goal is to find the root of all thoughts staying therein. Her again asking the same query "Who am I?" constitutes the search of a scientist. As a result there is a sudden surge of knowledge, stimulation of latent knowledge that is concealed within.

Yoga and IQ – Development at the Mental Level

Yoga and IQ are closely interlinked and development at the mental level through Yoga therapy is growing day-by-day.

All man's thoughts are chanelized through the process of concentration. This is the job of the intellect. The next thing to do is focus one's mind on a single thought.

This, in Yoga therapy is called Dharana and effortless

Dharana becomes meditation, Dhyana. All the 3 stages, Dharana, Dhyana and together with the next step Samadhi help cultivate better IQ. According to Yoga, there is an essential difference between IQ development methods in the intellectual and mental levels. At the intellectual level, understanding becomes the key to IQ. At the mental level, memorization happens by remaining with a single thought through repetition of the same thought over and over again. This is done through the relaxed, effortless process of dhyana.

A person can enter into Samadhi of one's own accord, or develop a photographic IQ as the end result. In Superconsciousness comes the process of what is called Sanyama by which one is able to unravel that knowledge which is hidden deep within the subtler layers of one's IQ.

Yoga therapy techniques include various ways of meditating. Some of these are Transcendental meditation, OM Meditation, Yoga Nidra and Trataka. All these help in Dharana and Dhyana that lead up to Samadhi.

Yoga therapy has also come up with a set of games and songs that help enhance the IQ at these levels. Breathing exercises (pranayama) are also widely used to cultivate a better IQ. Some of them include, Kapalabhati, sectional breathing and other sorts of breathing exercises that help improve IQ.

1. Deepening perception: Yoga therapy helps the mind function optimally.

   Yoga therapy helps do this through stimulations (Yoga cleansing kriyas) and Yogic relaxation (Shavasana and Pranayama).

2. Cutting down distractions and raising one's attention span: Yoga therapy exercises aim to eventually reaching a state transcendence of the mind. One feature of this state is to be able to modify and adjust mind functions by will power.

3. Awakening latent areas: capabilities practices help awaken latent areas, thereby giving the individual more capabilities and power. Interestingly, even celebrated geniuses make use of only up to 10% of their total brain capabilities. Most normal people make use of less than 5% of total brain potential.

4. Filtering positive memories from negative ones: Ideally, our IQ development should help a person achieve the very source of one's thoughts and our existence. In Yogic parlance this is called the Anandamaya Kosa. The way to do this is to substitute negative thoughts that generate displeasure with constructive ones.

Yoga Therapy to Improve IQ

Anyone can improve his / her by practising Kapalabhati (40 – 50 strokes a min), Anuloma-Viloma (9 – 10 rounds),) and Brahmari (10 rounds). You can use this Yoga capsule any number of times during the day, preferable thrice a day. These Yoga therapy practices clear all unwelcome, distressing and disquieting thoughts. In turn the make the mind clear, so that whatever you see and understand will ultimately soak into deeper layers of the IQ system.

■ ■ ■

Chapter 10

Music and IQ

Experiments have revealed that people sometimes enjoy a brief improvement in visual-spatial skills immediately after listening to a Mozart sonata. However, the results have been inconsistent, with some labs reporting that they were unable to reproduce the effect. It's also unclear if it's really the music that is responsible for the temporary enhancement of intelligence. It seems more likely that people improve their performance because listening to music elevates their mood and leaves them feeling more alert.

Brain scanning technologies have permitted neuroscientists to test ideas about the link between music and intelligence. Musicians have distinctively different brains. For instance, if you examine the brain of a keyboard player, you'll find that the region of the brain that controls finger movements is enlarged.

Moreover, brain scans of 9- to 11-year old children have revealed that those kids who play musical instruments have significantly more grey matter volume in both the sensorimotor cortex and the occipital lobes.In fact, musicians have significantly more grey matter in several brain regions, and the effects of music lessons seem to increase with the intensity of training.

One study compared professional keyboard players with amateurs. Although both groups had music training, the professionals practiced twice as much. The professionals also had significantly more grey matter volume in a number of brain regions.

In the Genes?

It's not simply a case of genetics—i.e., that people with more grey matter volume are more likely to become musicians. Research suggests that the brains of non-musicians change in response to musical training.

In one study, non-musicians were assigned to perform a 5-finger exercise on the piano for two hours a day. Within five days, subjects showed evidence of re-wiring. The size of the area associated with finger movements had become larger and more active.

So it's reasonable to think that the brain grows in response to music training. Does these brain differences reflect differences in intelligence?

Maybe so.

In the study of 9 to 11-year olds, musicians performed better on several tests than did their non-musical peers. They scored significantly higher on tests of vocabulary and finger tapping.

They also exhibited a strong, but statistically non-significant, trend towards better spatial and math skills.

And other studies reveal a variety of notable—and statistically significant —differences in test scores between musicians and non-musicians.

Music and Intelligence

Musicians perform better on cognitive tasks.

People with music training often outperform their non-musical peers on cognitive tasks.

For instance, a study of 4 to 6-year olds found that musically-trained kids performed better on a test of working IQ.

Other research indicates that musicians perform significantly better on tests of

- Spatial-temporal skills
- Math ability
- Reading skills
- Vocabulary
- Verbal IQ
- Phonemic awareness

Musically-trained people perform better on general intelligence tests.

In a cross-sectional study of Canadian school children, E. Glenn Schellenberg found that kids who took music lessons had slightly higher IQs. The effects were general, cutting across several different intellectual abilities (e.g., verbal, mathematical, and temporal-spatial). Music lessons were associated with abilities associated with fluid intelligence, such as

- Working IQ
- Perceptual organization
- Processing speed

They were also associated with increased verbal comprehension and better high school grades.

These differences remained significant after controlling for a child's age, nonmusical activities, family income, and parent's education.

As noted by Schellenberg and other researchers, a variety of explanations might account for it. For example, music lessons might enhance intelligence because they train kids to

- focus attention for long periods of time
- decode a complex symbolic system (musical notation)
- translate the code into precise motor patterns
- recognise patterns of sound across time
- learn rules of pattern formation
- memorise long passages of music
- understand ratios and fractions (e.g., a quarter note is half as long as a half note)
- improvise within a set of musical rules

All of these explanations have in common the idea that music lessons cause higher IQs.

But there is also the 'killjoy' hypothesis—the idea that music lessons are the effect, not the cause, of higher IQs.

Maybe parents with higher IQs are more likely to enroll their kids in music lessons. Or maybe kids with higher IQs are more likely to seek out and stick with music lessons because they find music training more rewarding. The best way to rule out the inheritance explanation is to perform controlled experiments, randomly assigning kids with no prior music training to receive lessons.

Several studies have pursued this approach. The results are intriguing.

Evidence that music training is the cause—not merely the effect—of higher IQ

One study randomly assigned 4-year olds to receive either weekly keyboard lessons or a control condition for 6-8 months. The kids who received music training performed better on a test of spatial skills. These results were replicated by other research.

Another experimental study randomly assigned 6-year-olds to receive one of four treatments during the school year:

- Keyboard lessons
- Vocal lessons
- Drama lessons
- No lessons

By the end of the school year, all participants experienced an increase in IQ. However, the kids who received music lessons showed significantly more improvement than the other groups did.

These results support the idea that musical training causes improvement in IQ. But, as E. Glenn Schellenberg points out, we don't know long the effect will last and at least one music training experiment has failed to find a link between music and intelligence.

One problem, says Schellenberg, is that a lot of people drop out of these experiments before they are completed. More long-term studies should help clear thing up.

One such study is being conducted by Gottfried Schlaug and his colleagues at the Music and Neuroimaging Laboratory at Beth Israel Deaconess Medical Center and Harvard Medical School.

These researchers are tracking the effects of music lessons—specifically, piano and violin lessons—on brain development and cognition.

Fifty kids, aged 5 to 7 years, began the study with no prior music training. Before starting music lessons, these kids were given brain scans and cognitive tests to establish baselines. Researchers are also following a control group, matched for age, socioeconomic status and verbal IQ.

One year into the study, the musically-trained kids already showed greater improvement in fine motor skills and auditory discrimination skills. Although there were no other statistically significant differences between groups, the musicians also showed trends for

- a greater increase in grey matter volume, and
- greater improvement on verbal, visual-spatial and math tests

Schlaug and colleagues are betting that these trends will become statistically significant over time. They'll continue to track these kids for many years. For more information about their continuing research on music and intelligence, check out their website.

Music and Intelligence: The bottom line

Nobody rules out the idea that genes may contribute to some of the IQ advantage enjoyed by musicians. But researchers strongly suspect that music training is responsible for some of the effect. In the next few years, we may have definitive evidence on this point.

At the same time, we shouldn't overlook the obvious: Music lessons are intrinsically rewarding. When kids learn to play a musical instrument, they are laying the groundwork for a lifetime's appreciation of music.

Effects of Music

The Mozart Effect

1. The most well-known study of classical music effect's

on IQ produced what was quickly coined 'the Mozart Effect'. Although generally taken to mean that listening to Mozart would improve one's IQ, this is actually rather misleading.

In fact, the 1993 study only showed that 36 college students who listened to 10 minutes of Mozart a day were better at spatial temporal exercises (things like knowing what a sheet of paper would look like unfolded) afterward than after listening to either nothing or relaxation music.

This falls short of scientific proof that listening to Mozart makes a person smarter overall, especially given the miniscule sample size.

2. Another commonly overlooked factor is the difference between learning music, such as playing an instrument or reading sheet music, and merely listening to it.

   A 2005 study conducted over the course of a year, the results of which were published in the neurological journal "Brain," did show that after studying music, children had developed better IQ and cognitive skills.

3. In "The Mozart Effect: Can listening to music really improve your child's IQ?" an article published on the BBC Web site, Dr. Alexandra Lamont from Keene University is quoted as stating, "There's no evidence that just listening to music, not learning to play an instrument, has any effect at all with children or with babies."

4. Many of the studies involving children who had cognitive improvement after learning about (not just listening to) classical music do not show whether the improvement would continue after several years. Other studies have found

that improved cognition after listening to classical music is only temporary, and still other research has yielded evidence that no cognitive improvement results at all.

5. The scientific community has reached a general consensus that learning to play a musical instrument or studying music will be beneficial and will not do any harm, even if it is only in terms of teaching discipline and time management.

Moreover, the visual and space orientation capacities have been shown to improve for a short while (10-15 minutes) after listening to music, this is part of the Mozart effect. The name itself "Mozart effect" came from the fact that it is believed that intelligence levels are increased by listening Mozart's compositions.

However, from merely listening to further studying music, the step is considerably important and consequently the results follow! Simple listening differs significantly from the actual learning to play an instrument or sing. Why so?

In the process of learning music the brain modifies, it actually enlarges within certain areas connected with this particular task.

Studies and brain scans have revealed that the musicians' brain is different; for example a piano player has got more gray matter in the region that controls the fingers' movement.

In the study named "The Effects of Musical Training on Structural Brain Development several scientists namely Krista L. Hyde, and Alan C. Evans (from Montreal Neurological Institute, McGill University), Jason Lerch from (Mouse Imaging Centre, Hospital for Sick Children, Toronto, Ontario, Canada),Gottfried Schlaug, Andrea Norton, and Marie Forgeard (from the Department of Neurology, Music and

Neuroimaging Laboratory, Beth Israel Deaconess Medical Center and Harvard Medical School) and Ellen Winner (from the Department of Psychology, Boston College, Chestnut Hill, Massachusetts, USA) have brought relevant insight with their study.

They investigated the structural changes that occur in the brain as a result of 15 months of instrumental music teaching on young children; this group was compared to a group of children that did not have musical training.

As expected, the children who participated in the music training showed improved finger moving and rhythm task yet the tasks that did not involved musical field remained the same. The gray matter development has been also observed in areas other than those directly connected with music namely – hearing and finger moving.

The complex process of learning produces growth in other parts of the brain and these facts lead to the idea that long-term programs of brain training may well help neuron growth in children. This is particularly relevant for children with developmental problems as well as for grownups with neurological conditions.

Musicians generally have grayer matter compared to non musicians and he also has shown that children who play instruments have also a significant increase of gray matter.

What's more, when professional and amateur musicians are compared, it is clearly revealed that the professionals who actually practice twice as much have again, more of a brain development than the amateurs.

It is than obvious that brain development can be associated with learning music, yet is this development only significant for music related tasks or is it relevant in other tasks as well?

Studies conducted on musicians and non-musicians bring

light upon a diversity of differences, some notable and some statistically proven. A testing on cognitive tasks shows that musician usually do better than their non-musical peers when it comes to cognitive tasks.

Also increased IQ levels have been noticed in musically trained children with ages between 4 to 6 years old when compared to the non-musical children of the same age.

Here is a list of tasks where it has been observed that musically trained people perform better: vocabulary, math, reading, verbal IQ, space orientation skills and phonemic awareness.

Another study shows that musically trained school children got better results on IQ tests. Several intellectual abilities are connected to music learning and seem to have a beneficial influence in developing musicians' IQ in areas connected to fluid intelligence like the speed of processing, verbal comprehension, working IQ and perceptual organization.

IQ was measured with standard tests before and after training. The effect was small, with a rise of just 7 IQ points for the keyboard and voice groups, compared with 4 in the drama and control groups.

The so called Mozart effect refers to the finding that passive listening to Mozart pieces temporarily ameliorates spatial abilities. Researchers propose that a 10 min, listening to Mozart arouses positive moods, accounting for the mentioned improved performance.

However it is important to remember that Mozart effect is not a wonder drug. It just improves your overall cognitive arousal and concentration. If you are looking to utilise music as a way to boost IQ long-term, it is important to learn to play an instrument.

Music researcher Donald Hodges says scans of the brain (while actively playing music) show both hemispheres (i.e. left and right sides of the brain) lighting up "like a pinball machine".

Fact file:

- One study found students with music training scored 52 points higher on the verbal portion and 37 points higher on the math portion of the "old" SAT than students with no such training
- Another study found learning music at an early age leads to long term gains in math and science reasoning skills
- The Mozart Effect: listening to a Mozart sonata (or other complex music) can temporarily increase IQ by 8 to 9 points

Presumably, music lessons would increase musical aptitude, as well as the nonmusical abilities associated with aptitude. Indeed, research unravels that music lessons have positive associations with verbal IQ spatial ability, reading ability, selective attention and mathematics achievement.

Music learning involve extended periods of rapt attention, dedicated daily practice, reading musical notation, memorization of long musical passages, learning about a variety of musical structures (e.g., intervals, scales, chords, chord progressions) and progressive mastery of technical (i.e. fine-motor) skills and precision in expression of emotions in performance.

Several researches concur that music lessons improves the IQ. This positive impact on cognition, is remarkably distinct, particularly during the childhood years, when brain development is highly tensile and sensitive to environmental influence.

A new study found that taking music lessons in childhood

was a significant predictor of a higher IQ in early adulthood. For the newbie adults, the study found a positive association between music lessons and higher school grades and higher scores on achievement testing in mathematics, spelling and reading.

As for the college freshmen, a history of playing music regularly as children and teenagers had " little but significant" associations with IQ, perceptual organization, working IQ and average high school grades, with the associations remaining significant after controlling for differences in family income, parent's education levels and gender

Jill Mattson in her upcoming book throws light on the power of sounds. According to Mattson "Listening to special sounds is a sure fire way to boost your intellectual capacities". She reports that, intellectual abilities, a function of frequency of his or her brain, keep fluctuating several times during a day. "Some brain wave frequencies can boost people's academic capacities," she said. "The good news is that specific sounds hold the power to alter people's brain waves, enabling us to access our peak intellectual performance whenever we want to."

■ ■ ■

CHAPTER 11

IQ Quizes

Mathematical Intelligence

We all require some numerical skills in our lives, whether it is to calculate our weekly shopping bill or to budget how to use our monthly income. Flexibility of thought and lateral thinking processes are a few skills which are needed in order to solve these problems. Mathematical intelligence generally represents your ability to reason and to calculate basic arithmetic computations. It also helps you to understand geometric shapes and manipulate equations. Mathematical intelligence is a strong indicator of general intelligence because many every day mental tasks require arithmetical operations even though numbers may not be involved.

1. Which number should come next in this series?

   25,24,22,19,15

A. 4

B. 5

C. 10

D. 14

Answer: C

Explanation: The pattern decreases progressively: -1, -2, -3, -4, -5

2. Which number should come next in this series?

   3,5,8,13,21,

A. 4

B. 21

C. 31

D. 34 Answer: D

Explanation: 3+5=8, 5+8=13 and so on.

3. Which number should replace the question mark?

   17 8 5 5

   13 7 5 4

   6 12 6 3

   10 6 4 ?

A. 4

B. 5

C. 6

D. 7 Answer: A

Explanation: (For each row the sum of the first two columns is equal to the multiple of the last two columns)

4. Which number should replace the question mark?

   8 5 21

   35 32 12

   32 28 31

   4 ? 28

A. 3

B. -2

C. -6

D. 48 Answer: C

Explanation: (For each row subtract the second column from the first column. The result is equal to the sum of the digits in the last column.)

Verbal Intelligence

It is said that to have a mastery of words is to have in one's possession the ability to produce order out of chaos and that command of vocabulary is a true measure of intelligence. Verbal intelligence measures your capacity to use language in order to express yourself, comprehend stories and understand other people. Verbal abilities include reading, writing and communicating with words. The verbal component of this test examines your vocabulary and your capacity to learn verbal material. It also measures your ability to employ verbal skills in reasoning and problem solving.

1. Rearrange the following letters to make a word and choose the category in which it fits.

   RAPETEKA

A. city

B. fruit

C. bird

D. vegetable Answer: bird (parakeet)

2. Find the answer that best completes the analogy

   people : democracy :: wealthy :

A. oligarchy

B. oligopoly

C. plutocracy

D. timocracy

E. autocracy Answer: plutocracy

3. Find the answer that best completes the analog

languages : meaning :: philology :

A. erudition

B. philosophy

C. ethics

D. semantics

E. grammar Answer: semantics

4. Which one of the sets of letters below can be arranged into a five letter English word.

A. A T R U N

B. P O D E B

C. R N A S L

D. M O H A T

E. E T L R N Answer: R N A S L (snarl)

5. What is the missing letter?

A. E C O

B. B A B

C. G B N

D. D B ? Correct answer: H

Explanation: Convert each letter to its numerical equivalent in the alphabet e.g. the letter "C" is assigned the number "3". Afterwards, for each row, multiply the numerical equivalents of the first two columns in order to calculate the letter in the third column.

6. Find two words, one from each group, that are closest in meaning.

   Group A

   raise

   floor

   stairs Group B

   top

   elevate

   basement

A. raise and elevate

B. raise and top

C. floor and basement

D. stairs and top

E. floor and elevate

Answer: raise and elevate

Spatial

Spatial abilities are the perceptual and cognitive abilities that enable a person to deal with spatial relations, in other words the visualisation and orientation of objects in space. Put simply spatial skills assess your ability to manipulate 3D objects by flipping and rotating them. Spatial intelligence questions test raw intelligence without the influence of prior knowledge and as such performance on this scale is indicative of general intelligence. At a first glance, such questions may appear daunting but the trick is not to give up too quickly. Often a second look at the problem will reveal a different approach, and a solution will appear because the brain has been given the opportunity to process information further. 1. Which diagram results from folding the diagram on the left?

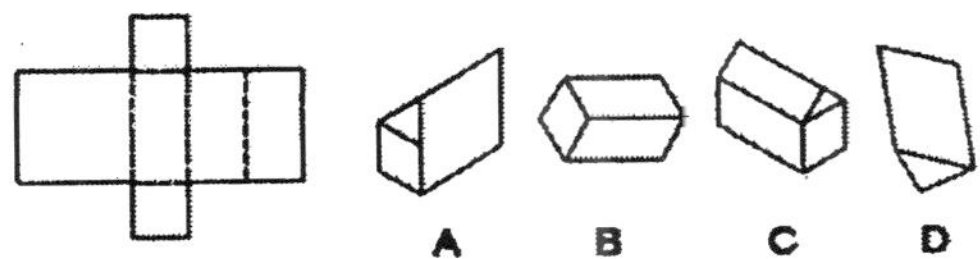

Answer: A

2. Which of the cubes is the same as the unfolded cube below?

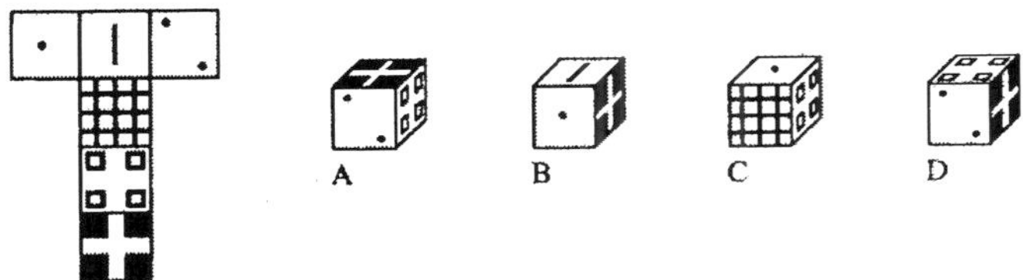

Answer: A

3. Which one of the Rubik's cube below can be part of the sequence?

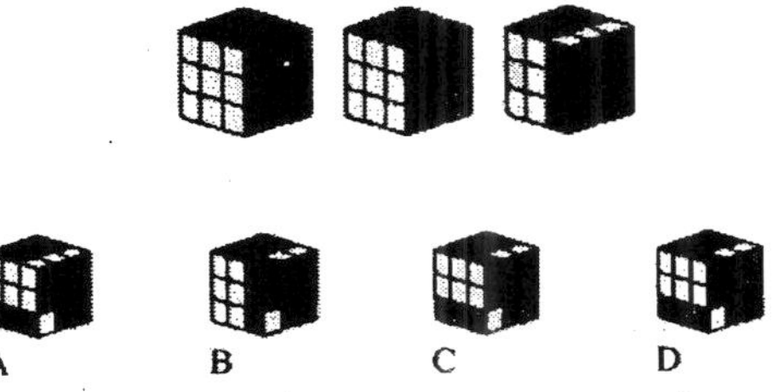

Answer: C

Visualization

Visual intelligence measures the ability to process visual material and to employ both physical and mental images in thinking.

As a result people with a high visualisation IQ find it easier to comprehend information and communicate it to others. Your visualisation skills determine how well you perceive visual patterns and extract information for further use. Visualization also facilitates the ability to form associations between pieces of information something which helps improve long-term IQ.

1. Pick the piece that's missing from the diagram below:

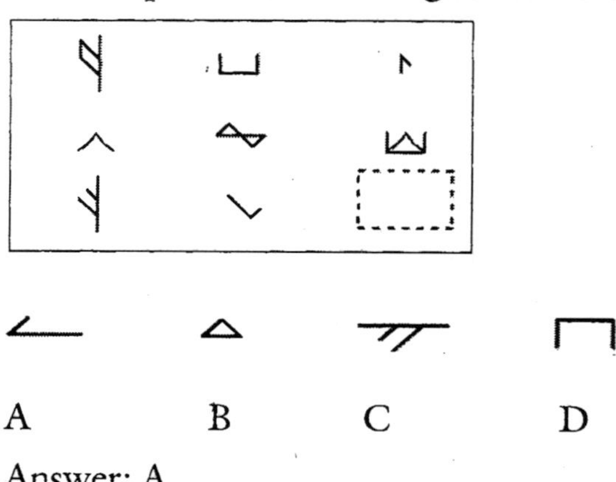

A B C D

Answer: A

2. Which figure is the odd one out?

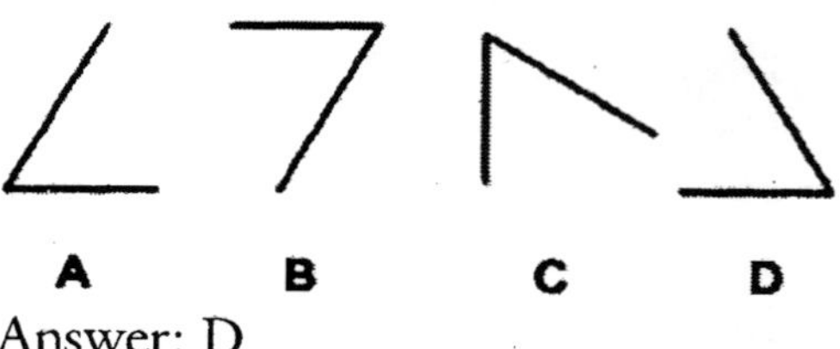

A B C D

Answer: D

3. Which of the following figures is the odd one out?

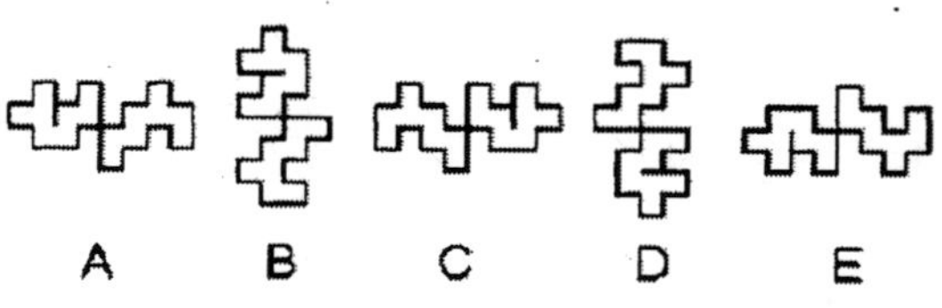

A B C D E

Answer: A

4. Which of the following figures is the odd one out?

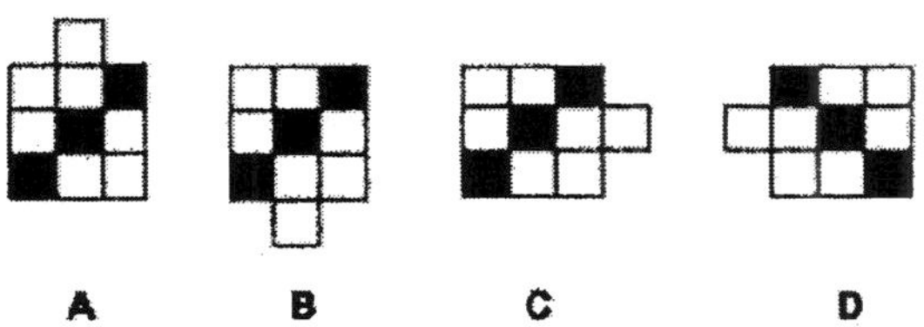

Answer: C

5. How many four sided shapes does this diagram have?

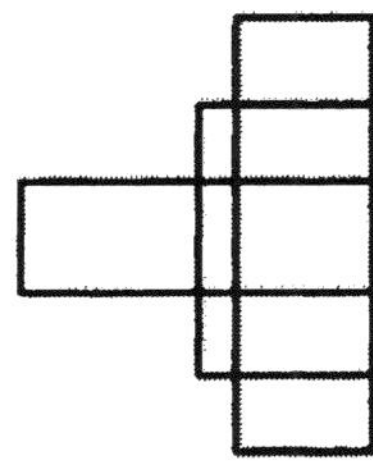

A. 5-10

B. 11-15

C. 16-20

D. 21-25

E. 26-30

Answer: E

Classification

This intelligence is closely related to the concept of general intelligence and measures the ability to organise collections of items by finding similarities and differences between them. By grouping together items such as words, ideas, songs or pictures you are able to achieve a more conceptual understanding of the relationships between them. Classification skills enable you to discern relevant data and this helps you gain a better general understanding of the world.

1. Which word does not belong?

   apple, marmalade, orange, cherry, grape

A. apple

B. marmalade

C. orange

D. cherry

E. grape Answer: B

2. Which number does not belong?

4	32	144
17	28	122
18	64	188
322	14	202

   Answer: 17

   Explanation: 17 is the only odd number.

3. Which of the following diagrams is the odd one out?

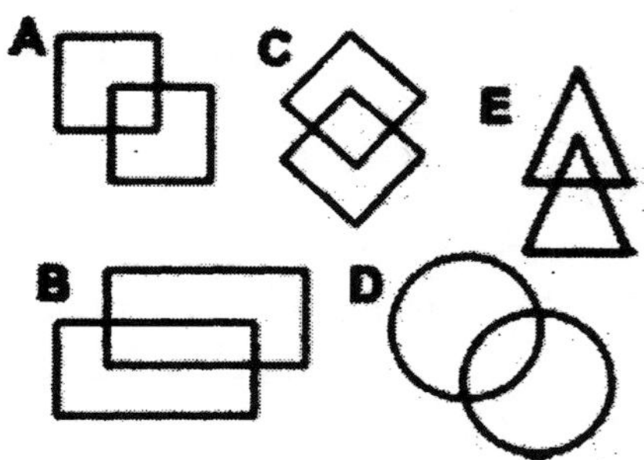

Answer: D

Explanation: D is the only diagram where the intersection does not form the original shape.

Logic

Logical thinking is the ability to make deductions that lead rationally to a certain conclusion. It is important to have good logic skills because they help you think things through and they also give you a good understanding of cause and effect relationships. In this test your logic IQ was assessed through your ability to comprehend and follow certain rules and conditions set forth in many of the questions.

Generally speaking logic skills make divergent thinkers and have proven to be very successful in our daily lives. Furthermore when combined with social insight and and self awareness logic skills make us into effective human beings. Improving these skills will increase your IQ and give you a good base for academic and personal success.

1. At the end of a banquet 10 people shake hands with each other. How many handshakes will there be in total?

A. 100

B. 20

C. 45

D. 50

E. 90 Answer: C

2. The day before the day before yesterday is three days after Saturday. What day is it today?

A. Monday

B. Tuesday

C. Wednesday

D. Thursday

E. Friday Answer: E

3. Select the number that best completes the analogy

   10 : 6 :: 3 : ?

A. 2

B. 1

C. -1

D. 12

E. 4 Answer: -1

4. Which number should come next in the series

   1, 3, 6, 10, 15,

A. 8

B. 11

C. 24

D. 21

E. 27 Answer: 21

5. 165135 is to peace as 1215225 is to

A. lead

B. love

C. loop

D. castle Answer: love

6. Library is to book as book is to

   Binding Copy Page Cover

A. page

B. copy

C. binding

D. cover Answer: page

Pattern Recognition

Out of all mental abilities this type of intelligence is said to have the highest correlation with the general intelligence factor, g. This is primarily because pattern recognition is the ability to see order in a chaotic environment; the primary condition for life. Patterns can be found in ideas, words, symbols and images and pattern recognition is a key determinant of your potential in logical, verbal, numerical and spatial abilities. It is essential for reasoning because your capacity to think logically is based on your perception of the logic around you. Your pattern recognition skills are expressed verbally through your long term exposure to language and your mathematical and spatial abilities are based on your perception of numerical data and 3D objects

1. Find the picture that follows logically from the diagrams to the right.

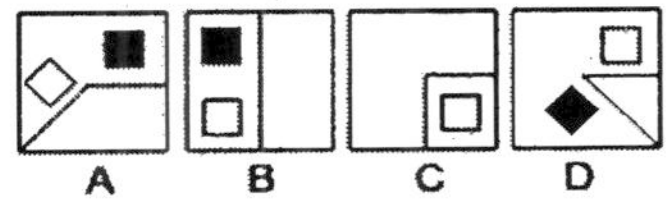

Answer: A

2. Find the picture that follows logically from the diagrams to the right.

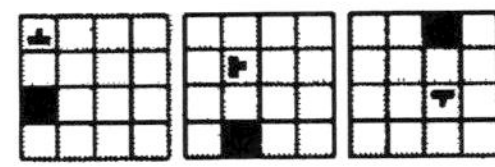
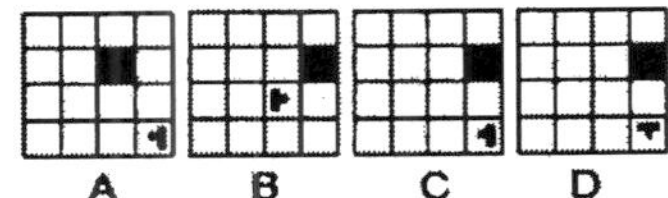

Answer: C

3. Please enter the missing figure: 4, 5, 8, 17, 44,

A. 80

B. 125

C. 112

D. 60

E. 84 Answer: B

Explanation: The difference between the numbers follows the series 1,3,9,27,81

4. Please enter the missing figure: 13, 57, 911, 1315, 1719

A. 2123

B. 1879

C. 3002

D. 5004

E. 1784 Answer: A

Explanation: All odd numbers in a series.

5. Which of the diagrams follows?

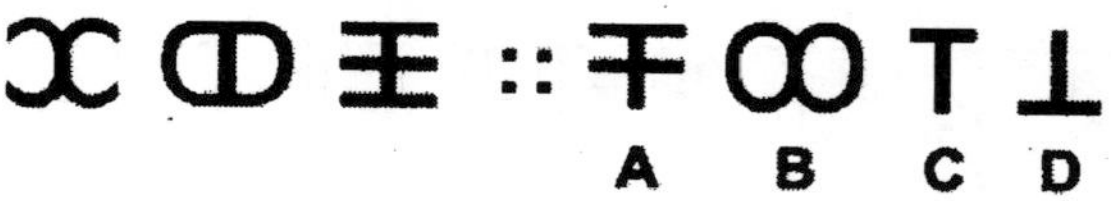

A B C D

Answer: A

Explanation: All the characters are letters back to back (C,D,E,F)

CHAPTER 12

IQ and Myths

Here are some common myths associated with IQ along with evidence that negates them:

Myth: IQ can measure intelligence

This is the first and the most common IQ myth. Majority of the people tend to confuse themselves between IQ and intelligence.

Reality

A person is said to have a high degree of intelligence if he or she can quickly adapt to new surroundings and act according to the immediate demands of the new situation. If that person is successful in overcoming all the hurdles and in the process acquires some specialized knowledge from which he can benefit immensely in his future, he is declared as an intelligent person. Intelligence is just a relative term. It cannot be measured. On the other hand, IQ is a "measure of relative intelligence which is determined by a single or a set of standardized test." IQ is a mathematical ratio.

Myth: IQ is fixed; it doesn't change

The second most common IQ myth is that a person's IQ never changes. People who are found to be academically poor in their childhood are tagged as one with low IQ for the rest of their lives.

Reality

Since IQ is a ratio, the number changes depending on what a person learns. A study at Michigan University led by Swiss post-doctoral fellows Susanne M. Jaeggi and Martin Buschkuehl has revealed that at least one aspect of the IQ – a person's fluid intelligence can be improved. Fluid intelligence depends upon short-term memory. The researchers gathered four volunteering groups and provided them with auditory and visual cues that they were supposed to store and recall. The training session would be held for half an hour after a gap of several days. The researchers found that the volunteer's fluid intelligence would go up after every session.

Myth: IQ depends fully on the genes of a person and is hereditary

This is also a popular myth. People have this misconception that IQ is solely the product of good genes. A child born out of parents having low IQ will also have low IQ. Besides, they also believe that this IQ will never change.

Reality

We all know that IQ comes from a combination of both genetics and environment. Experts believe that the genes affect our IQ by 40 to 80 percent and the remaining comes from external environment. Now, just think what will happen if a person is kept in isolation from all external stimuli? What will be the proportion of their intelligence coming from the environment? Obviously zero! Isn't? Hence, the more stimuli a person gets from the world, the more is their intelligence based on the environment. It is, thus, proved that IQ is not fully depended on the genes and it does change based on the environment. Besides, studies have also found significant increase in IQ from one generation to the other. It increases 21 points on an average in 30 years.

Myth: IQ is restricted to a single parameter of intelligence

Since there many types of intelligence and some people are good at something and some bad in that thing, most people have proclaimed that IQ is just restricted to a particular type of intelligence.

Reality

IQ covers all types of intelligence. It deals with the general mental ability. Research has shown that different types of intelligence are highly correlated and IQ measures this relative intelligence. In short, smart people tend do well on most tasks, while a dull person fails to do most of those tasks.

Myth: IQ is a racist term and minorities have low IQ

This is a myth prevalent mostly among the minorities who unfortunately have low IQs. These people have unanimously declared that IQ is a racist term used for discriminating the minorities.

Reality

We all know that IQ is not entirely genetic and is very much dependent upon the surrounding environmental changes. Low IQs of the minorities are more likely a result of discrimination in education and the atmosphere in which they have grown up. It has nothing to do with Europe or Asia, White or Black,

Christians or Jews etc. It is always possible that a white person can have a low IQ and a black a high IQ and vice-versa.

Myth: IQ is not important; it doesn't matter at all!

This is the last and the most deadly myth of IQ. Many people have this false notion that IQ is not required for success in life. Success depends more on personality, motivation and hard work.

Reality

Personality, motivation and hard work are needed for success in all our endeavours, but these are primary requirements. The basic and the most important requirement for success is at least an average IQ. It is IQ that is the best predictor of a person's capabilities.

Moreover, it is hard to measure motivation while personality measures can be faked. Generally, it is IQ that is incredibly used for choosing employees at work place or students at a school. Hence, IQ does matter and one has to work upon it.

Myth: IQ never Changes?

Reality

Another common misconception is that your IQ never changes. If people took an IQ test more often they would see the average American IQ changed.

Because your score is a ratio, your IQ score changes in relation to what you know and learn throughout your life.

For example, if you take a test in the 28 age group when you are 21, then take it again three years later your score cane go either up or down depending on the level of life experiences, learning, and education you have in the interim.

Myth: IQ is Genetically Relevant

Reality

Many people believe your IQ is genetic. Many assume because both parents have a low IQ so will their children, and vice versa. Both genetics and the environment a child grows up in influence IQ. It is not accurate, but up to 80 per cent of the American IQ is hereditary with the remainder derived from external stimulations. IQ is dependent on the level of external stimulus it receives as it develops and cannot solely depend on genetics.

Myth: You can only be Intelligent in one Area

Reality

There is a misconception that if you do well in one area of intelligence then you cannot do well in others. Intelligence quotient covers all aspects of your intelligence so, in fact, highly intelligent people tend to do well on all the tests and a mentally challenged person will tend to do poorly on them all.

Myth: IQ as a Racist Term

Reality

Many claim that IQ is a term that discriminates against minorities.One explanation for this is that people with low IQs from other countries use this as an excuse. Possibly this is true. More likely though is that the tests are written for the average American IQ and cultural, environmental, educational, religious, and social differences are not allowed for in tests taken by non-US citizens.

Myth: Intelligence Quotient has no Importance

Reality

These days, people tend to believe intelligence quotient is not important for success and that it is more important to have motivation, personality, and be prepared to work hard.These are all needed for success in conjunction with your IQ. And for basic success in life you need at least an average IQ. If you have a less than average IQ, you start to fall into the mentally retarded categories and no amount of hard work, motivation, or personality will make you successful without the IQ to learn basic life skills.

Myth: The Title of the IQ Test

Reality

It is rather unfortunate that psychologists haven't till now frozen on a system to compare two IQ scores from two varying tests. Comparing two scores just on the basis of their magnitude may not be a very good idea. To determine if a score is good you have to know what the test is about and what was the highest score that one secured.

Myth: How tough is the test?

Reality

The second parameter to be focused on is how tough the IQ test it. It will be easy to know if the score is really good, if we know how tough is the test. Usually the tougher the test is the lower one scores. It is highly probable that the IQ scores of two tests with the same name differ. This is because the level of difficulty of both the tests is not the same. Those who design the test decide upon the level of difficulty depending upon the age group, education and other parameters.

Myth: The Matter matters

Reality

There can be a lot of tests which have the same title or name but have different matter or subject they focus on. A 120 IQ score on one test, say verbal capability doesn't mean you have the same level on a test with the same name but focus on mathematical abilities. Usually IQ tests try to include subject from all other categories, but today IQ tests are becoming more and more focused. Hence the subject of focus of the test should also be given its due consideration.

Myth: Age: Another Parameter to be addressed

Reality

When you are young, you tend to be a high IQ scorer. As you grow up the intelligence start deteriorating. But the actual intelligence that you possess may be different. The label of test, the level of difficulty or the focus area of the test is crucial. The highest score that you have got in any IQ test may not be the correct indicator of your intelligence.

Myth: Standard Deviation Units may differ

Reality

Mental age was believed to be good enough to evaluate your intelligence. But soon it was found to be of no use and a concept of intelligence quotient (IQ) was born. It is ratio of mental age to chronological age interpreted in percentage. 100 is believed to be an average score and any difference is believed to be above of below average. This system was good until it was proved worthless, because the standard deviation is not the same throughout your life.

Myth: IQ Score: does it exist?

Reality

No digit cannot be established as a good IQ score. Any such claim is false and biased. So there neither exists a good IQ score or a bad one for that matter.

But the industry is not at all concerned to remove this

misconception. No efforts are being taken to clarify this issue by anyone.

Myth: The final number, given by IQ test results, is the indicator of your intellect and abilities

Reality

Eysenck's Test consists of several sections (so-called subtests) for abstract, verbal, figurative thinking, etc. The subtests results are summarised, and an averaged mark is given according to their results. Consequently, for example a person with great figurative thinking has a low logical thinking thus the IQ-test final result will be so-so.

Myth: The higher the IQ, the smarter its holder is

Reality

Indeed, IQ score is an indicator human's abilities to learn something new. This is the extent to which people can observe and understand what is going on. But it has nothing to do with practical mind or creative abilities.

Myth: A person with a high IQ is more likely to succeed in life than others

Reality

In the preface to one of his most popular editions of IQ-test Eysenck wrote that in order to achieve success in life the high levels of intelligence must necessarily be accompanied by persistence and high motivation. A person with high intellect but devoid of perseverance risks spending his life in the anticipation of "his hour". An unwearying in cognition but unmotivated person risks not leaving his sofa. Sadly, the greatest chance of success has the combination of perseverance plus motivation, even if there is no bright intelligence.

Myth: If your IQ is above 170, you are a genius.

Reality

The highest score for IQ professional tests is 144. The result that exceeds this number is not much detailed, falling between 150 to 160 or 160 to 170, etc. However, the precise results are always given by Eysenck's posted in Internet.

Myth: You can test yourself in Internet and know your own IQ level

Reality

All tests posted in Internet are the simplified versions of Eysenck's questionnaire. If such a test scored you 171 with a note Congratulations, you are indisputably a genius, it should necessarily be added: on the background of third graders. Professional IQ-test is revised by psychologists once in a couple of years also taking into account the Flynn effect.

Myth: IQ – A constant Value.

Reality

First, it is necessary to distinguish between real intellect and IQ-test indicators. The real abilities may vary slightly depending on the mood, well-being and even self-esteem.

Regarding the tasks of the test, we should always remember: the situation, in which the tested occurs, is somewhat artificial. A person may understand the badly formulated or badly translated task conditions wrong. As a result he may lose his interest towards this task in the midst of the test or just be inattentive. On the other hand, you may be trained to solve Eysenck's test tasks so that they will bounce off the teeth. However, this will not be the indicator of your overwhelmingly increased intellect.

Myth: You Will Experience Mental Decline As You Grow Older

Reality

This is a total myth with no basis in reality. Mental decline only happens when you fail to use your mind in the way it was intended. If you keep yourself mentally active and fit for most of your life, you will keep your mental functions in tip top condition right into old age. In fact, people who keep mentally active throughout life are generally in better mental shape than much younger people who fail to do this.

Myth: You Cannot Increase Intelligence

Reality

This is another very popular misconception which has been floating around for decades. Intelligence can be increased, because it isn't fixed at all. It is true to say that the number of neurons doesn't increase - because it doesn't need to. It is the number of glial cells which your brain has which determines how smart you are. So, go after glial cell growth, rather than brain/neuron cell growth. It is in the changing number of glial cells that high levels of intellectual ability can be achieved.

Myth: The Most Important Thing To Determine IQ Is Genetics

Reality

This, once again is another misconception. Genetics only counts for about 50% of your IQ level. Genes do play a part, so if you have very smart parents, you are more likely to be smart yourself. However, genetics on its own can in no way determine your full mental ability. There are many other huge factors which can influence it such as background, diet, behavior and similar. These 3 account for the remainder of your IQ ability.

■ ■■

Other Books on
QUIZ & CAREERS